*rea*discover...

BooksMusic**Film** Information **Cor**
Family history   Mag
Faxing**Games****Children's storytir**

renew th

b

projects for small gardens

projects for small gardens

56 projects with step-by-step instructions

Richard Bird

George Carter

photography by
Jonathan Buckley
Marianne Majerus
Stephen Robson

RYLAND
PETERS
& SMALL

LONDON NEW YORK

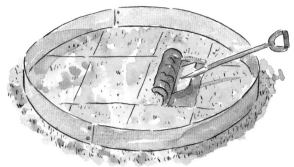

B 79 138 6 42 5

For this edition:

Senior designer Sally Powell

Senior editor Clare Double

Picture researcher Emily Westlake

Production Paul Harding, Deborah Wehner

Art director Anne-Marie Bulat

Editorial director Julia Charles

Illustration David Atkinson, Richard Bonson,
Martine Collings, Tracy Fennell, Valerie Hill,
Stephen Hird, Sarah Kensington, Sally Launder,
Amanda Patton, Elizabeth Pepperell, Lizzie Sanders,
Helen Smythe, Ann Winterbotham

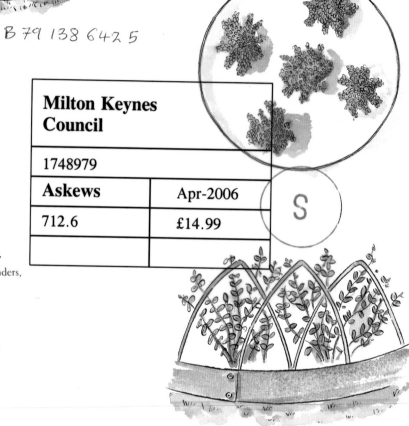

First published in the United Kingdom in 2002
This edition published in 2006
by Ryland Peters & Small
20–21 Jockey's Fields
London WC1R 4BW
www.rylandpeters.com

10 9 8 7 6 5 4 3 2 1

Text © Richard Bird 1998, 2000, 2002, 2006
and George Carter 1997, 2002, 2006
Design, illustrations and photographs © Ryland
Peters & Small 1997, 1998, 2000, 2002, 2006

ISBN-10: 1-84597-123-X
ISBN-13: 978-1-84597-123-6

A CIP record for this book is available from
the British Library.

Printed and bound in China

3550

contents

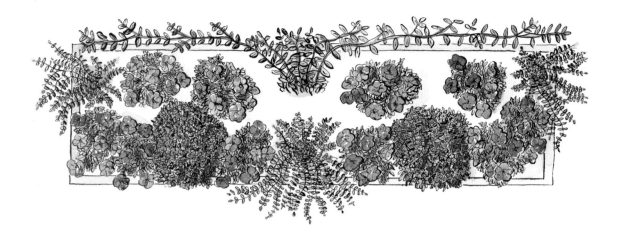

Designing or redesigning even the smallest garden can appear daunting when considered as a whole, but if it is approached as a series of projects the prospect at once seems more manageable. Of course, you need to devise an overall plan for a garden before attempting individual projects – but, once this has been done, then each area can be tackled in your own time.

Many of the projects in this book add a structural element that would suit any small garden, whether formal or informal or natural in character. Most gardens can benefit from containers that provide year-round focal points, such as the Versailles Case shown on pages 14–17, especially when planted up with an evergreen shrub. Taller structures such as arches and arbours also play an important role in small gardens by meeting the need for height when the space for trees is limited. The Vertical Planting project illustrated on pages 120–23 shows how to make the most of walls for growing plants when space for horizontal planting is restricted.

In addition to projects involving building or construction, there are plenty of ideas for exciting and unusual planting schemes, both decorative and edible, in beds or containers, some of which are suitable for a back yard, a balcony or even a window sill.

containers to make

a wood and trellis camouflage box

This container is designed to mask plants in plastic pots for seasonally changing arrangements. There is no base – simply fit it over your potted plants. A useful disguise for pots, this box also enables you to mix plants with different soil and feeding requirements.

MATERIALS & EQUIPMENT

2 pieces exterior-grade plywood 600 x 380 x 20 mm (24 x 15 x ¾ in)

2 pieces exterior-grade plywood 560 x 380 x 20 mm (22½ x 15 x ¾ in)

4 pieces planed softwood 750 x 50 x 50 mm (30 x 2 x 2 in)

13.6 m (44 ft) length of 25 x 10 mm (1 x 1½ in) planed softwood for trellis

1 litre (1¾ pints) each clear wood preservative and matt emulsion paint

sherardized panel pins 50 mm (2 in) and 25 mm (1 in)

waterproof PVA glue

no. 8 screws 50 mm (2 in)

16 standard-sized bricks

4 marguerites (*Argyranthemum frutescens*) in 250 mm (10 in) diameter plastic pots

1 To assemble the sides of the box, place the ends of the shorter boards against the inside face of the longer ones; glue in place, then reinforce with 50 mm (2 in) panel pins. Mark a line 50 mm (2 in) from the top all the way around the box; the trellis will be fixed below this line.

To apply the trellis to the outside of the box, follow steps 2, 3, 4 and 5 for each of the four sides.

2 Measure and cut a length of trellis to form a diagonal strut. Lay it against the side of the box with its centre line on the centre line of the diagonal. Mark and mitre the ends to match the corners of the box. Repeat for the other diagonal but cut a piece from the middle of the strut to fit. Glue and pin with 25 mm (1 in) panel pins.

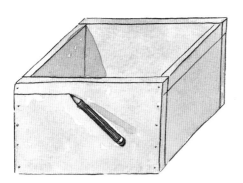

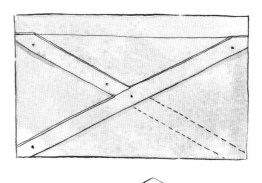

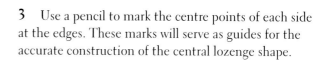

3 Use a pencil to mark the centre points of each side at the edges. These marks will serve as guides for the accurate construction of the central lozenge shape.

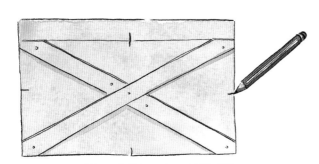

4 Make the first of the four lozenge struts by placing a section of trellis in a line from a top or bottom centre mark to a side mark. Cut a piece from the middle of this strut so that it fits around the latticework already in place, and mitre the ends.

5 Repeat step 4 for the other lozenge struts and fit them together on the box, matching the mitred ends. Pin and glue in place.

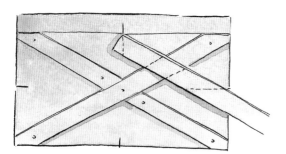

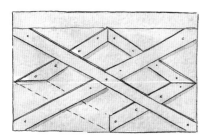

6 Treat the wood and trellis box inside and out with clear preservative and allow it to dry.

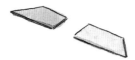

7 To form the top moulding, mitre the ends of the four pieces of pre-cut softwood so that they fit together snugly around the top edge of the box.

8 Prepare the box for the moulding by drilling holes for the screws along the top edges. Screw the moulding to the box from the inside so that it lies flush with the top edges. Reinforce the mitred corners with panel pins.

9 Apply two coats of matt emulsion in the colour of your choice to the inside and outside of the box.

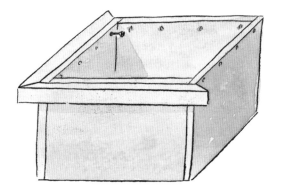

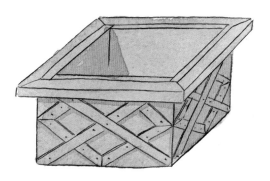

10 You may need to raise a platform to ensure that the tops of the pots rest just below the top of the moulding. In this project two layers of four bricks have been placed under each of the pots so that they sit 10 mm (½ in) below the top edge of the container; leave small gaps between the bricks to allow for drainage.

11 Place the plastic pots inside the container, one on each block of bricks. Marguerites have been picked for this display because their mass of foliage and flowers works well with the proportions of the box.

alternative planting schemes
Four *Fuchsia* x *speciosa* 'La Bianca'; 4 *Daphne odorata* 'Aureomarginata'; 4 common ivy (*Hedera helix* 'Erecta') around a common box (*Buxus sempervirens*); 4 bear's breeches (*Acanthus mollis*); 4 *Camellia japonica*.

a Versailles case

A Versailles case is a wooden box that was used at the Palace of Versailles in the 17th century for growing exotics such as oranges, lemons and palms, which could then be easily moved into the orangery and glasshouses for the winter. The great advantage of the Versailles case is that it can be unscrewed when the plants need repotting, or used as a decorative exterior for housing plants in plastic boxes or pots.

MATERIALS & EQUIPMENT

sawn timber (see step 1, page 16)

4 finials with 10 mm (½ in) diameter dowels or 4 wooden balls or pyramids with separate 10 mm (½ in) diameter dowels

square of exterior-grade plywood 375 x 375 x 10 mm (14¾ x 14¾ x ½ in)

no. 8 screws 50 mm (2 in) and 40 mm (1½ in)

waterproof PVA glue

1 litre (1¾ pints) wood preservative or oil-based primer

wood stain or matt emulsion paint

pot shards

50 litres moist compost

flowering tea tree (*Leptospermum scoparium*)

1 Cut the following pieces in sawn timber:
• 6 side boards 380 x 150 x 25 mm (15 x 6 x 1 in)
• 6 side boards 430 x 150 x 25 mm (17 x 6 x 1 in)
• 4 side supports 525 x 50 x 50 mm (21 x 2 x 2 in)
• 4 base supports 280 x 25 x 25 mm (11 x 1 x 1 in)

2 Prepare the shorter side boards by drilling two holes at each end 25 mm (1 in) in from the short edge, to fit the 50 mm (2 in) screws. Prepare the longer boards by drilling two holes at each end 50 mm (2 in) in from the short edge.

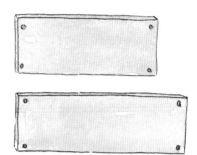

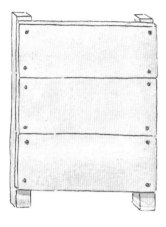

3 Using these holes, screw the shorter boards to the side supports, flush to the edge, with a 50 mm (2 in) projection at the bottom and a 25 mm (1 in) projection at the top.

4 Assemble the box shape by screwing the longer boards to the outside face of each of the side supports, creating a square-ended butt joint; use 50 mm (2 in) screws.

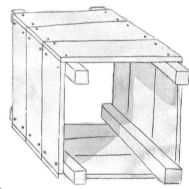

5 Prepare the base supports for 40 mm (1½ in) screws by drilling a hole about 25 mm (1 in) from each end. Place one support between each of the four side supports inside the box, positioning them at the base, flush with the bottom board. Screw in place.

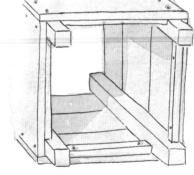

6 To fit the base, cut a 50 mm (2 in) square from each corner of the piece of plywood. Using a brace and bit, make five 25 mm (1 in) diameter drainage holes, positioning them as shown. Drop the base into the case from the top; it should rest on top of the base supports secured in the previous step.

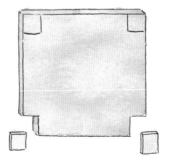

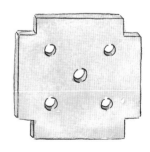

7 To attach the finials, drill a 10 mm (½ in) diameter hole for the dowel in the top of each upright, positioning it centrally. Use waterproof PVA glue to secure the finial in the prepared hole.

Alternatively, make your own finials, fixing them in place as above on a separate 50 mm (2 in) long dowel. Suitable designs for this size of case include a 50 mm (2 in) diameter wooden ball, or a 130 mm (5 in) high pyramid cut from a 50 x 50 mm (2 x 2 in) rod and sitting on a 25 x 30 x 30 mm (1 x 1¼ x 1¼ in) block.

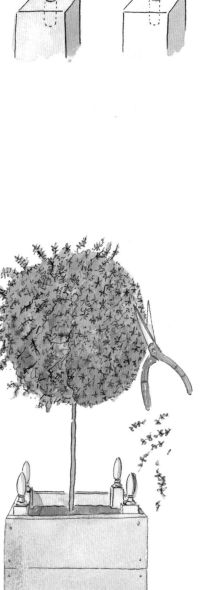

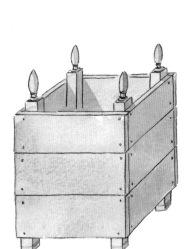

8 To protect the case, coat it in wood preservative inside and out. Then apply a wood stain or paint. Make sure the paint is thoroughly dry before planting up.

9 Line the base of the case with pot shards and enough moist compost so that the top of the potted plant sits 40 mm (1½ in) from the top of the container. Remove the plant from its pot and tease out the roots. Place inside the case and fill the surrounding space with the remaining compost to within 40 mm (1½ in) of the top. Firm loosely and keep well watered.

A flowering tea tree is pictured here, but Versailles cases are also suitable for large shrubs, topiary and masses of summer bedding.

10 After the tree has flowered, trim the outer leaves to keep the circular ball shape.

planted entrance containers

It is often useful to be able to raise plants high up so that they can be appreciated from a distance. Use the planters in pairs to resemble gateposts or as part of a screen to mark a division in the garden. These wooden gate piers have been designed as cachepots, so the individual plants remain in their plastic pots and can be changed seasonally.

MATERIALS & EQUIPMENT

1 sheet exterior-grade plywood 2400 x 1200 x 10 mm (96 x 48 x $\frac{1}{2}$ in)

2 squares exterior-grade plywood 290 x 290 x 10 mm (11$\frac{1}{2}$ x 11$\frac{1}{2}$ x $\frac{1}{2}$ in)

sawn timber or planed softwood (see steps 2, 3, 5 and 6 on pages 20 and 21)

exterior-grade wood preservative or oil-based primer

2$\frac{1}{2}$ litres (4$\frac{1}{2}$ pints) matt emulsion or microporous paint

waterproof PVA glue

sherardized panel pins 50 mm (2 in)

galvanized clout nails 40 mm (1$\frac{1}{2}$ in)

no. 8 screws 30 mm (1$\frac{1}{4}$ in) and 75 mm (3 in)

4 *Hydrangea macrophylla*

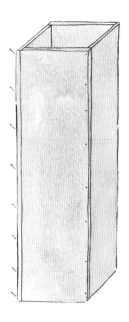

1 Cut the sheet of exterior-grade plywood into eight equal pieces, each measuring 1200 x 300 mm (48 x 12 in). Using square-ended butt joints, make two boxes by gluing the end of each board to the inside face of another; use panel pins inserted at a slight angle.

2 For the base supports cut four battens in sawn timber, each measuring 290 x 25 x 25 mm (11½ x 1 x 1 in). Position two battens on the inside of each box, opposite one another and 230 mm (9 in) down from the top. Drill holes in the plywood for 30 mm (1¼ in) screws. Glue the battens in place and secure with screws in the holes.

3 To make the top mouldings cut four pieces of sawn timber for each pier, 410 x 50 x 50 mm (16½ x 2 x 2 in). Mitre the corners to fit around the top outside edges. Glue and nail the mouldings in place flush with the top edge and finish by reinforcing the mitred corners with panel pins.

4 Treat the gate piers inside and out with clear wood preservative, making sure you coat the base thoroughly. When it has dried, apply two coats of matt emulsion or microporous paint to the outside and the inside down to the level of the base supports.

If the pier planters are to be placed on soil, follow step 5. To fix them to concrete or paving, follow step 6.

5 Make eight supporting stakes from sawn timber, each measuring 450 x 30 x 30 mm (18 x 1½ x 1½ in); sharpen one end on each until it forms a point. For each pier, knock four stakes into the soil, spacing them to fit into the inside corners; the internal dimensions of the pier are 290 mm (11½ in) square. Leave at least 150 mm (6 in) of stake above the soil. Lower each pier over the stakes to sit on the ground and check that the structure is vertical (a spirit level is useful here). If the surface is uneven, bank it up with soil so that the tops of both piers are level. Drill holes for 30 mm (1¼ in) screws in the bottom corners of the pier and then screw the stakes to the plywood structure.

6 To fix the pier to concrete, cut four battens from sawn timber, each measuring 290 x 50 x 50 mm (11½ x 2 x 2 in). Using two for each pier, place them opposite one another with the outside edges 290 mm (11½ in) apart. Rawlplug them for 75 mm (3 in) screws and, using a hammer drill with a masonry bit, secure them to the concrete. Slot the pier over the battens. Check they are level. Drill holes for 30 mm (1¼ in) screws and screw the pier to the battens through the sides.

7 Make the bases to hold the plants from the remaining squares of plywood. Drill five 25 mm (1 in) diameter holes through them for drainage purposes. Treat both squares with clear wood preservative before dropping them onto the supporting battens inside each pier.

8 The piers are now ready to be planted by placing the plastic container directly onto the wooden stage. Hydrangeas have been used for this project, but the height of the base and pier can be adjusted to suit plants of different size and shape.

alternative planting schemes
Other suitable plants for this arrangement include a box ball (*Buxus sempervirens*) or marguerites (*Argyranthemum frutescens*). You can adjust the height of the base and pier to suit the size and shape of your chosen plant. Keep all plants fed and watered according to their individual needs.

a trough with trellis screen

This versatile trellis-backed trough is essentially a portable container for tall plants and climbers and can be moved whenever you want to change your garden layout. It acts as both a screen and a planter and is ideal for use on a balcony or roof garden where it may be difficult to support posts.

MATERIALS & EQUIPMENT

sawn timber (see step 1 on page 24)

no. 8 screws 50 mm (2 in), 65 mm (2½ in) and 100 mm (4 in)

sherardized panel pins 40 mm (1½ in)

1 piece exterior-grade plywood 845 x 345 x 20 mm (33¾ x 13¾ x ¾ in)

13.7 m (45 ft) length of planed softwood for trellis 30 x 20 mm (1¼ x ¾ in)

1 litre (1¾ pints) wood preservative and 2½ litres (4½ pints) wood stain

pot shards

50 litres compost

1 *Trachelospermum jasminoides*

2 lesser periwinkles (*Vinca minor*)

3 sky-blue lesser periwinkles (*Vinca minor* 'Azurea Flore Plena')

10 *Petunia* 'Dark Blue Dwarf'

1 Cut the following pieces in sawn timber:
- 4 pieces for sides 350 x 150 x 25 mm (14 x 6 x 1 in)
- 4 pieces for front and back 900 x 150 x 25 mm (36 x 6 x 1 in)
- 4 side supports 300 x 50 x 50 mm (12 x 2 x 2 in)
- 2 base supports 750 x 25 x 25 mm (30 x 1 x 1 in)
- 2 base supports 250 x 25 x 25 mm (10 x 1 x 1 in)
- 2 trellis supports 1700 x 50 x 50 mm (68 x 2 x 2 in)

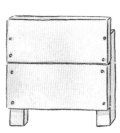

2 Drill holes for 50 mm (2 in) screws at both ends of the side boards. Use two boards for each side and screw them to the side supports, lining up the outer edges and staggering them so that two 50 mm (2 in) legs protrude from the bottom.

3 Assemble the box by screwing the front and back boards to the outside face of the sides; drill holes and use 50 mm (2 in) screws to secure the joint.

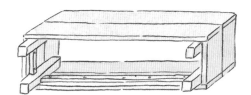

4 Drill the base supports for 50 mm (2 in) screws and slot the base supports between the side supports on the inside, flush with the base. Secure them in place with screws.

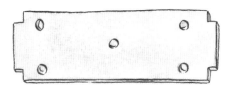

5 For the base, cut a 50 x 50 mm (2 x 2 in) square from each corner of the piece of plywood. Before dropping the plywood over the base supports, drill five 25 mm (1 in) diameter drainage holes.

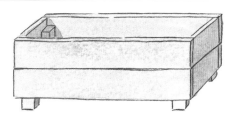

6 Treat the box and base with clear wood preservative. When it has dried, apply a couple of coats of stain.

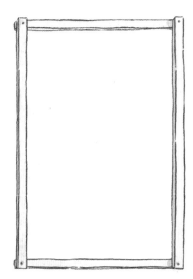

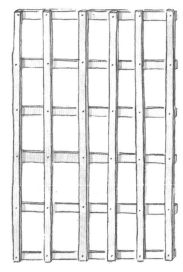

7 To make the trellis panel, cut the planed softwood into six sections measuring 1.35 m (54 in) and six measuring 900 mm (36 in). Start by making a rectangular frame: pin two of the shorter sections behind the longer ones, flush with the ends (far left).

8 Divide each side into five equal parts and mark the divisions with a pencil. Pin the vertical sections of trellis first, top and bottom, and then the horizontals behind these, pinning at all junctions. Treat the structure and the trellis supports with clear wood preservative (left).

9 Drill the trellis supports for 65 mm (2½ in) screws and place them against the back of the trellis, flush with the top and sides. Screw in place from the front. Stain the trellis and supports.

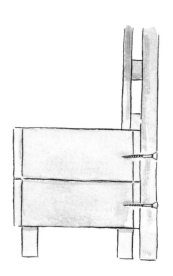

10 To join trough and trellis, drill holes in the trellis supports for 100 mm (4 in) screws; position the holes so that the screws will go through the trellis and the side supports inside the trough. Make sure that all sides and bottom edges line up and screw the pieces together.

11 Line the trough with pot shards and enough compost to ensure that the top of the plant sits about 25 mm (1 in) from the top edge. It is advisable to use a tall trained trachelospermum for this project; if your plants are small, it may be better to use two.

12 Place the plant in the centre at the back of the trough, tease out the individual stems and arrange them on the front of the trellis as evenly as possible; tie them to the trellis with coated wire.

13 Place the lesser periwinkles along the length of the trough and fill in the spaces with dark blue petunias. Add potting compost as you go, then firm in and water the trough. Use a liquid feed about once a fortnight.

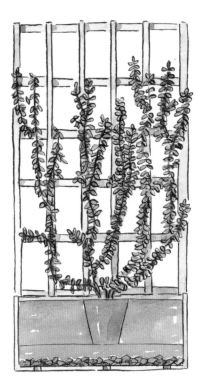

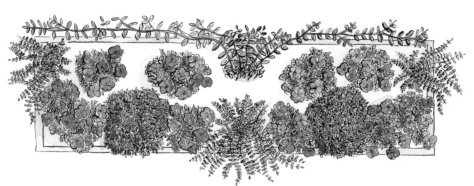

alternative planting schemes

For a colder climate, plant the semi-evergreen wall shrub *Pyracantha coccinea*, underplanted with *Hedera helix*. For the trellis backing you could also use a more hedge-like plant such as a hawthorn or holly or even the much despised *Aucuba japonica*, which thrives even in very polluted environments.

a herbal window box

This window box will give you the opportunity to cultivate herbs for the kitchen even in a very confined space. The colour scheme used here is based on golden sage, purple basil and cream oregano. If you prefer to grow other herbs, you can devise your own scheme – for example, a symmetrical planting scheme using a combination of shrubby and trailing herbs as well as a good contrast of colours creates a particularly decorative effect.

MATERIALS & EQUIPMENT

1 sawn timber window box 780 x 300 x 250 mm (31 x 12 x 10 in)

planed timber 1100 x 20 x 6 mm (43 x ¾ x ¼ in)

planed timber for moulding 1175 x 30 x 30 mm (46 x 1¼ x 1¼ in)

no. 8 screws 50 mm (2 in)

panel pins

waterproof PVA glue

1 litre (1¾ pints) clear wood preservative

1 litre (1¾ pints) wood stain (light green and grey umber mix)

50 litres soil-based potting compost

1 plastic pot

pot-grown herbs (see page 29)

1   This sawn timber window box can be bought from a garden centre or made at home. If you want to make the box yourself, see page 246, where the quantities and measurements of timber required are given.

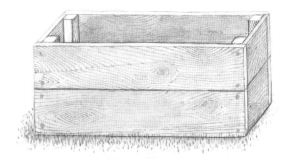

2   To attach the fretting, cut three 270 mm (10¾ in) vertical battens from the 20 x 6 mm (¾ x ¼ in) timber. Pin and glue them to the front of the box so that they sit 30 mm (1¼ in) from the top of the box. Cut four 360 mm (14½ in) battens to fit between the vertical battens.

3   To attach the cross fretting, cut four 450 mm (18 in) battens from the 20 x 6 mm (¾ x ¼ in) timber. Hold two of the battens in front of the box on the diagonal, as shown. Mark the pointed angles with a pencil so that the battens will fit within the vertical and horizontal battens. Cut, glue and pin in place.

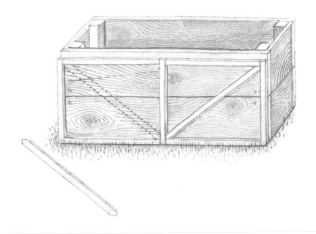

4   To create the crossed pattern, cut a further two 450 mm (18 in) battens. Cut them in half, and then cut them to fit, as in step 3. Glue, pin and wipe off any excess glue.

5   To make the mouldings, start by cutting four pieces of 30 x 30 mm (1¼ x 1¼ in) timber to the following lengths: one 840 mm (33½ in) for the front, one 780 mm (31 in) for the back, and two 310 mm (12½ in) for the sides. Leave the back and one end of the side mouldings straight; mitre all others (see page 247). Fix from the inside with 50 mm (2 in) screws. Apply wood preservative and stain.

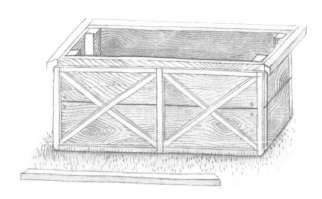

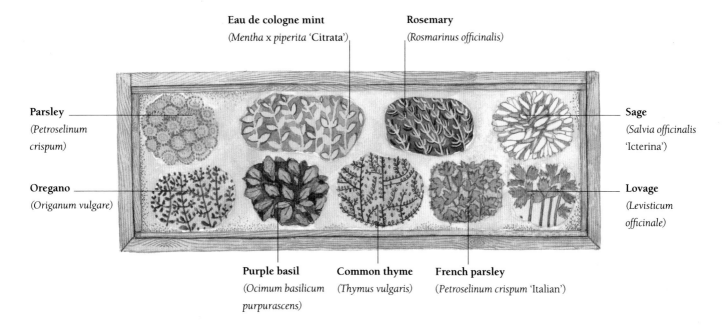

Parsley
(*Petroselinum crispum*)

Oregano
(*Origanum vulgare*)

Eau de cologne mint
(*Mentha x piperita* 'Citrata')

Rosemary
(*Rosmarinus officinalis*)

Sage
(*Salvia officinalis* 'Icterina')

Lovage
(*Levisticum officinale*)

Purple basil
(*Ocimum basilicum purpurascens*)

Common thyme
(*Thymus vulgaris*)

French parsley
(*Petroselinum crispum* 'Italian')

6 When the box is dry, fill it three-quarters full with potting compost and position the herbs as shown above. Keep the mint, which can be invasive, in a plastic pot and bury it in the compost. Top up the window box with the remaining compost and water thoroughly. Water and trim the herbs regularly.

a chamomile seat

Turf seats – consisting of a raised bed made from willow hurdles, bricks or timber planks – have their origins in medieval gardens. Planted with aromatic herbs, such as chamomile, or mown grass, they provide a pleasantly fragrant and comfortable seating area. Such seats were often placed in a niche or in a timber arbour festooned with sweet-scented climbers such as honeysuckle and roses. This seat is stained grey to simulate weather-bleached oak.

MATERIALS & EQUIPMENT

9.9 m (33 ft) sawn timber 150 x 25 mm (6 x 1 in)

2 m (80 in) sawn timber 50 x 50 mm (2 x 2 in)

2.8 m (112 in) sawn timber 25 x 25 mm (1 x 1 in)

no. 8 screws 50 mm (2 in) and 40 mm (1½ in)

exterior-grade plywood 1145 mm x 445 x 10 mm (45¾ x 17¾ x ½ in)

4 wood-turned finials 100 mm (4 in) tall with 10 mm (½ in) dowel

1 litre (1¾ pints) clear wood preservative

2.5 litres (4½ pints) grey umber wood stain

40–50 litres soil-based potting compost

52 pot-grown chamomiles (*Chamaemelum nobile*)

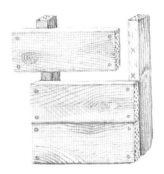

1   From the 150 x 25 mm (6 x 1 in) sawn timber, cut six 450 mm (18 in) side boards. From the 50 x 50 mm (2 x 2 in) timber, cut four 500 mm (20 in) posts. Drill holes in the corners of the boards, then fix the side boards to the posts using 50 mm (2 in) screws. Sand down rough edges.

2   From the 150 x 25 mm (6 x 1 in) timber, cut three 1200 mm (48 in) front boards. Drill holes in each corner of the boards and screw them to the two side panels. When you do this, turn the side panels on their sides to make the whole structure more stable.

3   From the 150 x 25 mm (6 x 1 in) timber, cut three 1200 mm (48 in) back boards. Drill holes and screw the three back boards to the two side panels. To do this, turn the whole structure over so that it rests on the front boards.

4   From the 25 x 25 mm (1 x 1 in) sawn timber, cut two 1050 mm (42 in) battens and two 350 mm (14 in) battens. Fix the battens to the upper boards of the front, back and side panels from the inside using 40 mm (1½ in) screws. Position the battens 110 mm (4½ in) from the top of the upper boards. The battens will then provide a good support for the plywood that will form the chamomile seat.

5 Drill fifteen 25 mm (1 in) diameter drainage holes in the piece of plywood. Use either a flat bit in an electric drill or a brace and bit. The holes should be spaced at intervals of 170 mm (7 in) lengthways and 90 mm (3½ in) widthways.

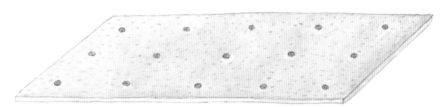

6 Cut a 50 x 50 mm (2 x 2 in) square notch from each corner of the plywood and slot into position on top of the supportive battens.

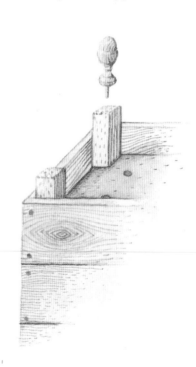

7 Drill a 10 mm (½ in) diameter hole in each of the upright posts and insert the decorative finials. Unless the wood has been pressure-treated, cover the finished seat with the wood preservative and paint with the grey wood stain.

8 Cover the seat base with a layer of compost. Arrange the chamomile plants in about two rows of twelve and two rows of fourteen. Fill in with the compost so that the surface is just below the top of the seat. Water the chamomile regularly and clip when uneven.

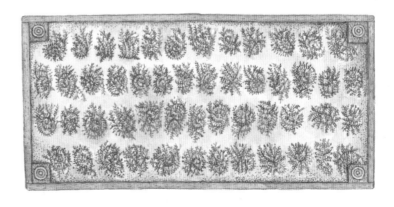

a raised scented window box

This scented window box is best placed below a window, from where the fragrance of the lavender, rosemary and thyme can drift into the room. You can adjust the height of your stand to suit the position of your window. Choose a window that enjoys a sunny position and keep the plants well watered, particularly in summer.

MATERIALS & EQUIPMENT

1 plywood window box 900 x 200 x 200 mm (36 x 8 x 8 in)

1 plywood rod 1400 x 25 x 25 mm (56 x 1 x 1 in)

planed timber 3000 x 50 x 50 mm (120 x 2 x 2 in)

planed timber 4050 x 50 x 25 mm (38 x 2 x 1 in)

planed timber 3400 x 40 x 25 mm (36 x 1½ x 1 in)

sherardized panel pins 40 mm (1½ in)

no. 8 screws 50 mm (2 in)

waterproof PVA glue

1 litre (1¾ pints) each clear wood preservative and grey matt emulsion

4 lead strips, 2 at 1450 x 90 mm (58 x 3½ in), 2 at 800 x 40 mm (32 x 1½ in)

nails 20 mm (¾ in)

soil-based compost

pot-grown herbs (see page 37)

tinsnips

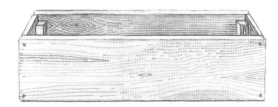

1 This plywood window box can be bought from a garden centre or made at home. If you want to make it yourself, see page 246, where the quantities and measurements of plywood are given.

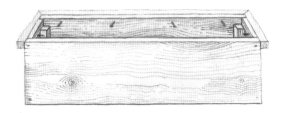

2 For the moulding, start by cutting two side pieces 230 mm (9 in) long and a front piece 950 mm (38 in) long from the plywood rod. Mitre one corner on each short piece and both corners on the long one (see page 247). Fit the moulding flush with the top of the box; glue and pin from the inside.

3 To make the stand, start by cutting four 950 mm (38 in) and four 250 mm (10 in) pieces from the 50 x 25 mm (2 x 1 in) timber. Mitre both ends of all the pieces. Glue and pin the joints.

4 Cut four 750 mm (30 in) legs from the 50 x 50 mm (2 x 2 in) timber. Drill holes in the frame corners and screw to the legs. Place one frame 10 mm (½ in) above the top of the legs and another 130 mm (5 in) up from the base.

5 For the lower shelf, cut two 800 mm (32 in) and two 900 mm (36 in) slats from the 40 x 25 mm (1½ x 1 in) timber. Arrange as shown over three 200 mm (8 in) supports. Position the outer slats flush with the supports and allow the inner slats to protrude by 50 mm (2 in) at each end. Pin in position.

6 Turn the stand upside down and slot the shelf into the bottom frame. Drill holes for the screws in the shelf supports and screw them to the legs. For added strength, insert pins into the supports from the outside of the frame. Unless the wood has been pressure-treated, apply wood preservative to the box and stand, and paint with two coats of matt emulsion.

7   Mark a line down the centre of one 1450 mm (58 in) lead strip. Mark two 250 mm (10 in) long sections at the sides. Divide the side sections into three equal parts and the central section into ten equal parts. Draw the scallops between these marks so that the top of the scallop meets the bottom edge of the lead. Cut out the pattern with tinsnips. Repeat for the second strip.

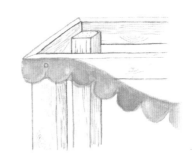

8   Nail one strip to each frame. Put the straight edge flush with the top edge on one side, fold to the front and planish the corner with a smooth-faced hammer. Nail the front in place, planish the other corner and nail down the other side.

9   Cut the ends of the last two lead strips into V-shaped notches. Fold over 150 mm (6 in) at each end and bend the central section into a semicircle. Mould to create the wavy effect. Mark three fixing points 25 mm (1 in) below the top moulding, one in the centre and two 50 mm (2 in) in from the ends. Nail the ribbons to the box, overlapping them where they meet.

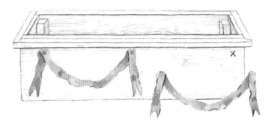

Lavender
(*Lavandula angustifolia* 'Hidcote')

Rosemary
(*Rosmarinus officinalis*)

Lavender
(*Lavandula angustifolia* 'Hidcote')

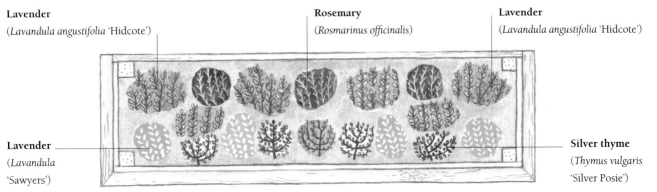

Lavender
(*Lavandula* 'Sawyers')

Silver thyme
(*Thymus vulgaris* 'Silver Posie')

10   Fill the base of the trough with compost. Unpot the herbs and position according to the planting scheme shown above. Work compost around the plants until the soil sits 25 mm (1 in) below the rim of the trough, then water thoroughly. The lower shelf can be used to display a row of painted pots of fragrant herbs that complement those in the window box.

balcony herb boxes

A roof garden, balcony or other small garden provides a perfect opportunity to grow herbs. These elegant boxes can be filled with herbs to create a gold, silver and purple display. You may wish to combine ornamental herbs with those for culinary use. Either follow the planting plans shown here or devise your own herbal colour scheme. These boxes have the advantage of looking decorative both from inside the house and from below.

MATERIALS & EQUIPMENT

4 planed timber window boxes 900 x 200 x 200 mm (36 x 8 x 8 in)

sawn timber 1530 x 25 x 25 mm (60 x 1 x 1 in) (optional)

1 litre (1¾ pints) clear wood preservative

1 litre (1¾ pints) dark grey undercoat

1 litre (1¾ pints) dark green gloss paint

8 galvanized roofing ties 600 mm (24 in)

24 roofing bolts 40 mm (1½ in) long with 6 mm (¼ in) diameter

peat-based compost

2 plastic pots 130 mm (5 in) in diameter

pot-grown herbs (see page 41)

lump hammer • metal vice

1   The window boxes can be bought from a garden centre or made at home. If you want to make them yourself, see page 246, where the exact quantities of wood are given. Unless the timber has already been pressure-treated, cover the boxes with clear wood preservative. Apply a layer of undercoat followed by a layer of dark green gloss paint.

2   You can also add two 230 mm (9 in) mouldings and one 965 mm (38 in) moulding cut from 25 x 25 mm (1 x 1 in) timber. See step 2 of the instructions for the window box on page 36 for cutting and attaching mouldings to the boxes.

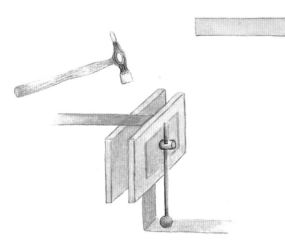

3   The brackets are purpose-made from galvanized roofing ties to fit the dimensions of the balcony rail, which in this case measures 130 x 50 mm (5 x 2 in). Mark two 200 mm (8 in) sections, one 130 mm (5 in) section and one 80 mm (3 in) section on each tie.

4   Bend the bracket into the correct sections in the metal vice, as shown, and use the hammer to sharpen up the edges. The brackets should fit the balcony rail well to make the boxes secure.

5   Paint the brackets with dark grey undercoat and then with gloss paint. Drill three 6 mm (¹⁄₄ in) diameter holes in each bracket and bolt the brackets to the box from the inside, as shown. To ensure that the boxes will fit back to back along the balcony rail, fix the brackets 100 mm (4 in) in from the ends of two of the boxes and 150 mm (6 in) in from the ends of the other two.

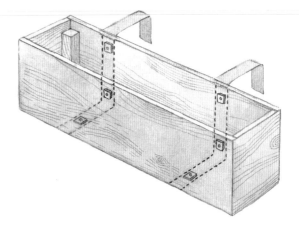

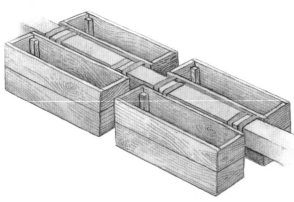

6   Hook the brackets over the balcony rail. The illustration on the left shows how the brackets on the boxes have been deliberately staggered to achieve a snug fit.

7 Fill the balcony boxes with compost so that the root ball of each herb sits 25 mm (1 in) below the top of the box. Plant the herbs according to the four planting schemes illustrated below. Plant the herbs in the larger pots first, then those in the smaller pots. Fill in with the rest of the compost and water well. Plant the peppermints in plastic pots to prevent them from spreading.

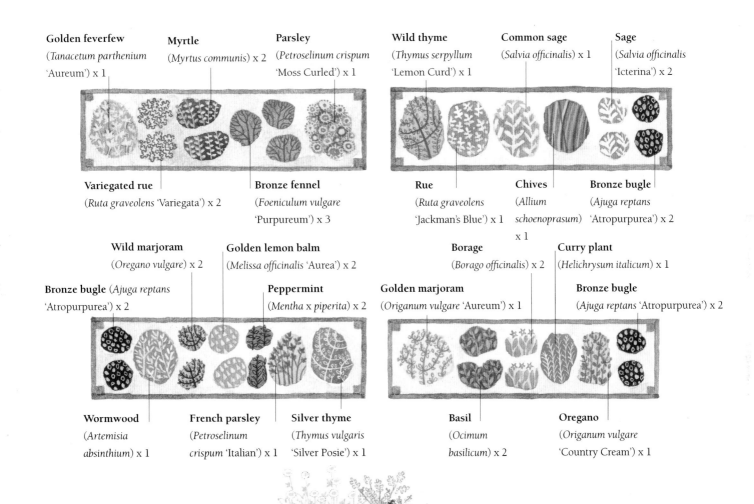

Golden feverfew
(*Tanacetum parthenium* 'Aureum') x 1

Myrtle
(*Myrtus communis*) x 2

Parsley
(*Petroselinum crispum* 'Moss Curled') x 1

Variegated rue
(*Ruta graveolens* 'Variegata') x 2

Bronze fennel
(*Foeniculum vulgare* 'Purpureum') x 3

Wild thyme
(*Thymus serpyllum* 'Lemon Curd') x 1

Common sage
(*Salvia officinalis*) x 1

Sage
(*Salvia officinalis* 'Icterina') x 2

Rue
(*Ruta graveolens* 'Jackman's Blue') x 1

Chives
(*Allium schoenoprasum*) x 1

Bronze bugle
(*Ajuga reptans* 'Atropurpurea') x 2

Wild marjoram
(*Oregano vulgare*) x 2

Golden lemon balm
(*Melissa officinalis* 'Aurea') x 2

Bronze bugle (*Ajuga reptans* 'Atropurpurea') x 2

Peppermint
(*Mentha* x *piperita*) x 2

Wormwood
(*Artemisia absinthium*) x 1

French parsley
(*Petroselinum crispum* 'Italian') x 1

Silver thyme
(*Thymus vulgaris* 'Silver Posie') x 1

Borage
(*Borago officinalis*) x 2

Curry plant
(*Helichrysum italicum*) x 1

Golden marjoram
(*Origanum vulgare* 'Aureum') x 1

Bronze bugle
(*Ajuga reptans* 'Atropurpurea') x 2

Basil
(*Ocimum basilicum*) x 2

Oregano
(*Origanum vulgare* 'Country Cream') x 1

8 Trim and prune all the herbs regularly to prevent them becoming overgrown. In late summer to early autumn, cut back the wormwood, rue, sage, myrtle and curry plant.

galvanized buckets

Hanging galvanized buckets on 'S' hooks is an inexpensive and attractive way of displaying plants. A bright and vibrant arrangement, such as the one used here, adds a splash of colour, decoration and movement to a blank expanse of wall in a simple setting. Pick similar flowers in sharp colours and bold shapes to contrast with the plain outline and shiny silver-grey surface of the buckets. For quick results, buy container-grown plants.

MATERIALS & EQUIPMENT

3 galvanized buckets 300 mm (12 in) in diameter

3 substantial galvanized angle brackets with tops 220 mm (8½ in) long and sides 250 mm (10 in) long

3 threaded eye bolts with nuts to fit the holes in the angle brackets

3 'S' hooks 80 mm (3 in)

no. 10 plated screws 50 mm (2 in)

pot shards

15 litres loam-based compost

4 African marigolds (*Tagetes erecta*)

2 pot marigolds (*Calendula officinalis*)

2 Artemisia 'Powys Castle'

2 single chrysanthemums

2 cone flowers (*Rudbeckia hirta*)

1   To prepare the buckets for planting, drill three drainage holes in the base of each one.

2   Line the bottom of each bucket with a layer of pot shards 25 mm (1 in) thick.

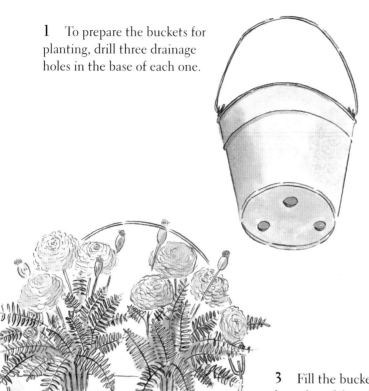

3   Fill the buckets about two-thirds of the way up with a loam-based free-draining compost. Then place four de-potted plants in each, making sure that the root ball is 25 mm (1 in) below the top edge of the bucket. Fill in with soil around the edges, lightly covering the surface of the root balls, and firm in. Give the plants a good soaking.

4   Choose a suitable location for your buckets. The plants used in this project need plenty of sun, so make sure your display area is in a sunny spot – a south-facing wall is ideal. Mark the position of each bracket on the wall with a pencil. In the example shown, the brackets have been staggered up a wall to allow space for plants to spread.

To fix the brackets to a stone wall, follow step 5.
To fix the brackets to timber clapboard, follow step 6.

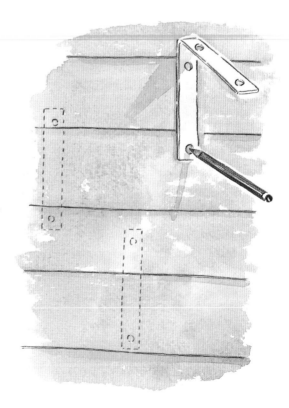

5 Screws and appropriate rawlplugs should be used for a masonry wall. Drill the holes for them with an electric drill and masonry bit.

6 For timber, use posidriv screws. If possible, fix the screws into a vertical studwork member behind the clapboard.

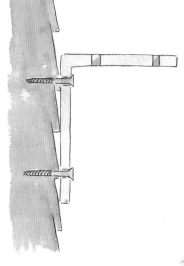

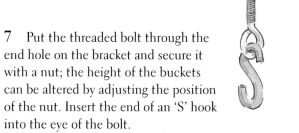

7 Put the threaded bolt through the end hole on the bracket and secure it with a nut; the height of the buckets can be altered by adjusting the position of the nut. Insert the end of an 'S' hook into the eye of the bolt.

8 This bucket has been planted with rudbeckias and chrysanthemums. It is especially important to keep all the plants well watered because the containers dry out quickly. Check daily if possible.

alternative planting scheme
Bring a burst of sunshine to a bare wall by filling your buckets with dwarf sunflowers (*Helianthus*), *Coreopsis tinctoria* and *Gazania* 'Orange Beauty'.

decorated
containers

a shell-faced trough

A simple decorative treatment refines the look of a concrete garden trough. Aluminium leaf adds a shiny surface to the shells but any metal leaf works well – the most extravagant-looking option being gold. Blue tones have been chosen for the planting arrangement since they complement the silvery-grey of the trough and shells. If you pick your own display, try to stick to one colour – a mixture may detract from the decorative impact of the container.

MATERIALS & EQUIPMENT

1 plain concrete trough 600 x 250 mm (24 x 10 in)

5 large scallop shells

1 litre (1¾ pints) dark grey undercoat

small jar Japan goldsize and aluminium leaf

paintbrush

two-part resin and hardener adhesive

30 litres potting compost

pot shards

pot-grown plants in 80–100 mm (3–4 in) pots, as follows:

5 *Delphinium belladonna* 'Wendy'

3 Cherry-pie heliotrope (*Heliotropium peruvianum* 'Royal Marine')

5 *Laurentia axillaris* 'Blue Star'

5 *Aptenia cordifolia* 'Variegata'

1   Paint the four sides of the trough and the first 25 mm (1 in) inside the top edge with the undercoat.

2   Pick five large scallops of roughly the same size; these can be purchased at a fishmonger's or a decorating shop. Clean and dry them thoroughly before applying the treatment. Paint the convex side with a single coat of undercoat.

3   When the undercoat on the shells has dried, paint over it with the goldsize. Wait until the surface is almost dry but still slightly tacky before attaching the metal leaf.

4   Apply the transfer leaf over the tacky surface of the shell; test that the adhesive is ready by placing a corner of the transfer onto the shell; if it instantly adheres, the shell is ready to take the leaf.

5   Attach the foil to the rest of the shell, rub it down lightly with cotton wool and peel back the transfer tissue. To achieve a distressed appearance, adhere the leaf to the raised areas of the shell; to do this, stretch the transfer over the upper surface and rub the top ridges only so that when you remove the backing the leaf has not stuck in the indents. Repeat for all five shells.

6   Mark the positions for the shells on the front and sides of the trough with a coloured pencil or a strip of masking tape; make your mark where the centre of the shell will sit. Site one shell centrally on each side of the trough and three spaced equidistantly on the front panel.

7   Now the trough and shells are ready to be joined. Mix the two-part adhesive – you will need an amount roughly the size of a golf ball. Using the applicator or a small wooden spatula, apply generous blobs of the glue to the inside edges of the shells in four or five places, as shown.

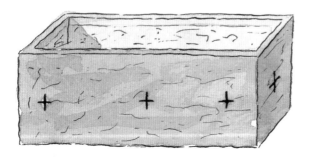

8 Tip the trough onto its side so that the front face is pointing upwards. Press each shell onto the three marked positions along the top and remove any glue spilling out from the sides with a clean applicator.

9 When the glue has dried, turn the trough back onto its base and fix the side shells; hold these in position while the adhesive sets.

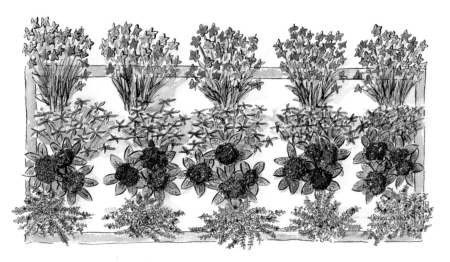

10 Put the trough in a sunny place and plant it up in June, using the scheme on the left as a guide. The plants have been positioned in rows and staggered to fit. The delphiniums are positioned at the back, followed by the laurentias; the heliotropes and the aptenias are along the front.

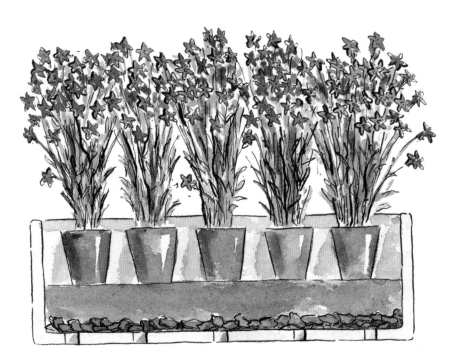

11 Cover the drainage holes with pot shards and fill the trough about half full with potting compost. Place the back row of delphiniums first and work your way forwards. Fill in with potting compost to within 25 mm (1 in) of the top edge, then firm in and water.

alternative planting schemes
For spring, plant *Convolvulus sabatius* with *Vinca minor* 'Alba Variegata'; in winter, fill the trough with winter-flowering pansies.

a lead-faced trough

Lead patinates to a beautiful silvery-grey colour – an effect that is simple and quick to achieve. You can simulate the appearance of a lead container by fixing sheet lead to a timber framework. Take care over size and placement; a window box must sit within the frame and be secured on brackets. Before embarking on this project, ensure that this style of container is in sympathy with the character and architecture of your building.

MATERIALS & EQUIPMENT

1 wooden box 950 x 250 x 230 mm (38 x 10 x 9 in)

2 pieces softwood 285 x 30 x 30 mm (11¼ x 1¼ x 1¼ in)

1 piece softwood 1030 x 30 x 30 mm (40½ x 1¼ x 1¼ in)

no. 8 screws 40 mm (1½ in)

galvanized clout nails 20 mm (¾ in)

clear wood preservative

1 bottle white malt vinegar

gauge 4 lead 1430 x 250 mm (57 x 10 in) and 1550 x 130 mm (62 x 5 in)

6 *Senecio cineraria*

5 *Petunia* 'Ruby'

4 *Osteospermum* 'Whirly Gig'

3 pink bellflowers (*Campanula carpatica*)

3 *Nemesia caerulea* • 3 Persian violets (*Exacum affine*)

tinsnips

1   Treat the box inside and out with wood preservative. Put on protective gloves before handling the lead, and wash your hands afterwards. Cut with tinsnips.

2   Attach the wider strip of lead to one side of the box, top and bottom, with the galvanized clout nails.

3   Wrap the lead round to the front and planish the corner with a mallet to achieve a sharp corner.

4   Nail the front in place, top and bottom, at 100–150 mm (5–6 in) intervals. Planish the other corner and nail the remaining side in place.

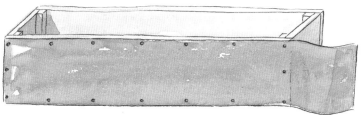

5   Take the three sections of softwood and mitre one corner on the short pieces and both corners on the longer one. Fit the sections together to form the moulding around the front and sides of the box, flush with the top edge. Drill holes for the screws around this edge and screw the moulding in place from the inside.

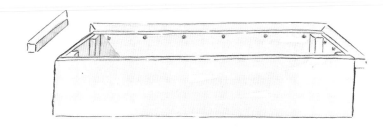

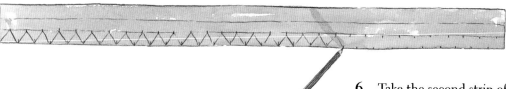

6   Take the second strip of lead and score a line along its length, using a nail and straight edge, 60 mm (2¼ in) down from the top. Divide the bottom into 31 sections of 50 mm (2 in), then divide the scored line into sections of the same size but starting 25 mm (1 in) in from the short end.

7 Join the marks up to form a zigzag pattern and then cut it out using tinsnips.

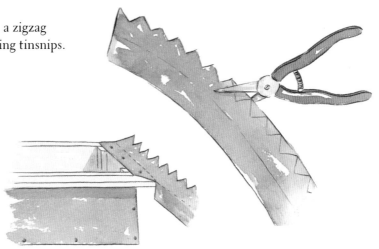

8 Place the straight edge of the strip along the inner edge of the box on the side. Nail it in place. To planish the strip neatly around the corner, cut out a 90° notch from the lead, making sure that the corner point lines up exactly with the corner of the moulding. Hammer down the zigzag edge on the side and wrap the lead to the front of the box.

9 Now planish the top of the front section so that the zigzag sits neatly along the outside of the moulding. Nail in place. Complete the lead facing for the last side, following the method already used.

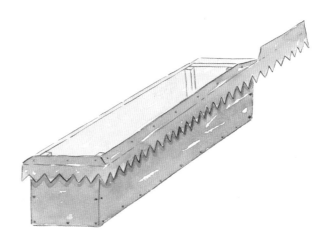

10 To give the box a patinated look apply white malt vinegar to the surface of the lead using a damp cloth. Keep applying until a mottled whitish-grey effect appears.

11 If your window sill slopes, make wedges to level the base of the box. Fix the box in place by screwing the inside of the box to the window frame or fixing retaining brackets to the front of the sill.

12 Line the box with pot shards and half fill with compost. Identify the plant positions by matching colours and numbers listed on page 52. Fill in with compost to 25 mm (1 in) below the top, firm in and water.

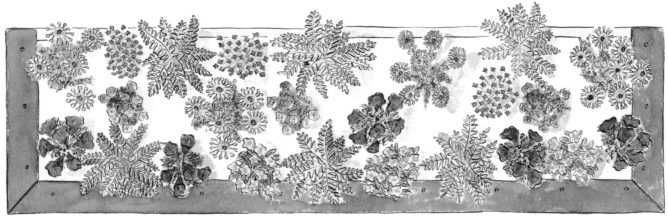

a rustic Regency window box

The fashion for producing objects covered in barked wood started
in the 18th century. This design is based on the style of the Regency
landscape gardener Humphrey Repton, who imitated the forms
of classical architecture using rustic materials such as barked
columns and pine-cone festoons.

MATERIALS & EQUIPMENT

exterior-grade plywood and planed softwood (see step 1, page 58)

1 litre (1¾ pints) each clear wood preservative and green wood stain

4 m (14 ft) halved barked poles with 50–65 mm (2–2½ in) diameter

3 large and 8 small pine cones

no. 8 screws 40 mm (1½ in)

galvanized clout nails 80 mm (3 in)

sherardized panel pins 50 and 65 mm (2 and 2½ in)

pot shards

30 litres peat-based compost

3 male ferns (*Dryopteris filix-mas*)

6 crested female ferns (*Athyrium filix-femina cristatum*)

9 white cup flowers (*Nierembergia*)

small bag of sphagnum moss

1 Cut the following in exterior-grade plywood:
• 2 pieces for front and back 900 x 250 x 20 mm (36 x 10 x ¾ in)
• 2 pieces for sides 160 x 250 x 20 mm (6½ x 10 x ¾ in)
• 1 piece for base 900 x 200 x 20 mm (36 x 8 x ¾ in)

Cut the following in planed softwood:
• 4 side supports 25 x 25 x 250 mm (1 x 1 x 10 in)
• 2 base supports 25 x 25 x 810 mm (1 x 1 x 32½ in)

2 Drill holes for screws in each corner of the side pieces and screw the side supports flush with the long edges.

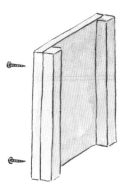

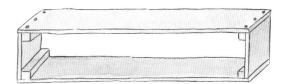

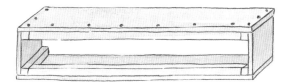

3 Drill holes along the short sides of the front and back pieces and place them flush with the outside edges of the side pieces. Screw in position.

4 Slot the base supports in between the side supports, flush with the base, and screw them in place through pre-drilled holes, front and back.

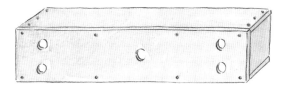

5 Drill five 25 mm (1 in) diameter drainage holes in the base, then screw the base to the bottom of the box, driving the screws into the base supports.

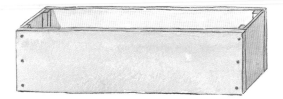

6 Coat the box inside and out with wood preservative. When it has completely dried, apply the green wood stain to the front, back and sides, on the outside only.

7 To decorate the front of the box, cut four sections of halved barked pole, two measuring 900 mm (36 in) and two measuring 250 mm (10 in). Mitre the ends of all four pieces, and using the 65 mm (2½ in) panel pins attach them to the front face; drive the pins in at an angle and make sure that all the corners meet.

8 For the sides, cut six sections of halved barked pole, each measuring 250 mm (10 in). Using three for each side, position the poles vertically and pin in place.

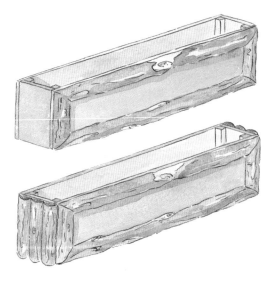

9 Cut one of the large pine cones in half lengthways with a hacksaw; use a vice to do this or pin one half of the cone to a board, which will hold the cone steady while you cut. With the tip facing downwards, pin the half-cone to the centre of the box using 50 mm (2 in) pins.

10 To complete the festoon effect, cut the small cones in half lengthways. Use a vice or construct a special cutting stand by pinning and gluing two pieces of 50 x 25 mm (2 x 1 in) timber to a plywood board, positioning them to fit the shape of the cone but leaving a gap at the top to allow for the saw. Push each cone between these rods and secure with galvanized clout nails, then cut in half with a hacksaw.

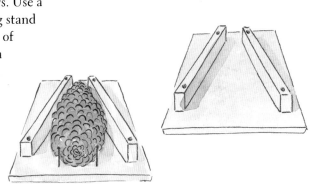

11 Draw two semicircles on the front of the box as a guide for the cone festoon. Pin and glue eight half cones to each semicircle; start at the top and place matching pairs opposite one another with the tips facing downwards – if your cones are slightly different sizes, place the largest ones at the top, graduating to the smallest at the central base of the festoon.

12 To construct the pine-cone finials, drill holes in the bottom of the two remaining large cones; make the holes big enough to accept half the length of the galvanized nails. Insert the nails and then cut off the heads with a hacksaw.

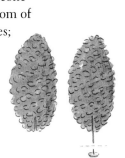

13 The finials are placed in the two side supports at the front of the box. Drill a hole for each finial and insert them; you may want to secure them further with a dab of PVA glue.

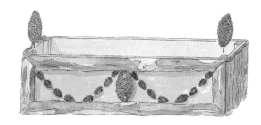

14 Line the base of the box with pot shards and half fill it with compost. Remove the plants from their pots and arrange according to the scheme pictured right, with the larger male ferns at the back. Add compost to 25 mm (1 in) below the rim, firm in and fill any gaps with moss before watering thoroughly.

15 Consider the positioning of the box carefully; ferns require shade and regular watering, although the moss will help to retain moisture. You could use white busy Lizzies (*Impatiens*) instead of cup flowers.

a circular pipe with flowering tree

In a paved garden or where soil is not available, large shrubs or small trees can be grown using inexpensive broad concrete pipes to contain the soil. Here a decorative niche gives height to the arrangement and frames the cascading flowers of the fuchsia.

MATERIALS & EQUIPMENT

1 section of concrete drainage pipe 500 mm (20 in) high
with a 900 mm (36 in) diameter

dark blue-green matt emulsion

pot shards

50 litres John Innes no. 3 potting compost

slow-release fertilizer

1 standard weeping *Fuchsia* x *speciosa* 'La Bianca'

10 lady's mantle (*Alchemilla mollis*)

6 pelargoniums (*Pelargonium* 'Friesdorf')

1   Choose a concrete drainage pipe to fit the size of the plant. The dimensions given on page 60 are suitable for a small to medium shrub. Conceal the rough surface of the pipe with a fresh coat of paint; dark blue-green harmonizes well with most garden schemes.

2   Position the painted pipe in your garden – it will rest equally comfortably on either a hard or a soft surface. Fill the base of the pipe to a depth of 30–50 mm (1–2 in) with pot shards; this will help to improve drainage.

3   If your weeping fuchsia is in a pot, carefully remove it and tease out any enmeshed roots. Fill the base of the pipe with enough compost to cover the pot shards. When you have finished planting, all the plants should be at the depth they were in the pots (see illustration to step 7). Add fertilizer as you plant.

4   Add compost to bring the plants and surrounding soil to a level about 40 mm (1½ in) below the rim of the pipe.

5   Place the fuchsia in the centre of the pipe. Again, the surface of the soil should be about 40 mm (1½ in) from the top of the pipe.

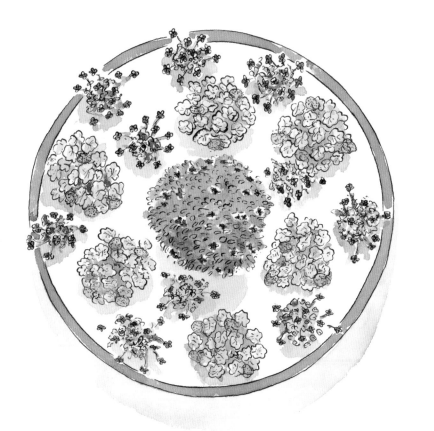

6 Underplant with lady's mantle and pelargoniums, placing them around the edge of the container in the positions shown left.

7 Pack the soil firmly around all the plants and water thoroughly. Monitor the container for water, especially during hot weather.

alternative planting scheme
Use two pipes of different diameters to achieve a stepped effect, inspired by medieval garden designs. Plant your tree in the central pipe and fill in the lower level with a seasonal planting scheme. This alternative planting display uses a weeping mulberry (*Morus alba* 'Pendula') above a bed of chamomile (*Anthemis nobile* 'Treneague').

a painted galvanized washtub

A galvanized tin or enamel bath can be turned into an elegant planter by adding ball feet to give it the look of an early-19th-century jardinière. This planter is good for a large mass of seasonal bedding and looks effective either on the ground or raised on a low plinth or wall.

MATERIALS & EQUIPMENT

1 oval tin bath 600 mm (24 in) long and 450 mm (18 in) wide

1 piece exterior-grade plywood 450 x 350 x 20 mm (18 x 14 x ¾ in)

4 turned wooden balls with 65 mm (2½ in) diameter and
4 separate 7 mm (⅜ in) diameter dowels 50 mm (2 in) long

waterproof PVA glue

small jar Japan goldsize

1 packet or twelve 50 x 50 mm (2 x 2 in) squares gold leaf or Dutch metal

½ litre (1 pint) each clear wood preservative and dark red undercoat

1 litre (1¾ pints) matt emulsion

30 litres John Innes no. 2 potting compost

bag of sphagnum moss

36 dwarf pink and red tobacco plants (*Nicotiana* Domino Series)

1   Begin by making a plywood base to fit the recessed stand underneath the tub; this forms a fixing for the feet. Mark the shape of the base onto the plywood.

2   Draw a second oval about 5 mm (¼ in) inside the first. Cut out the inner shape using a jigsaw.

3   Drill a 7 mm (⅜ in) diameter hole about halfway through each of the wooden balls, making sure it is straight and central.

4   Dribble a little glue inside these holes and insert the dowels so that they stick out about 25 mm (1 in) above the surface of the balls.

5   Paint the feet with clear wood preservative. When it has dried, apply two coats of dark red undercoat to simulate the colour of red gesso, which will give the finished effect a warm glow. Sand between each coat.

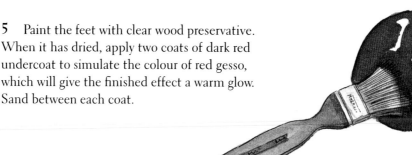

6   When the undercoat has completely dried, brush on a layer of goldsize. The goldsize needs to be almost dry to the touch before you apply the gold leaf. Place the gold leaf over the tacky surface of the balls. Smooth over the backing surface before carefully peeling it off, leaving a layer of gold.

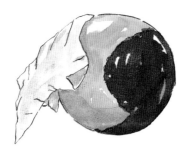

7   Continue to apply the gold leaf, overlapping subsequent sheets, until the entire surface of each ball is covered. Rub off excess gold leaf but don't worry if the surface is uneven – this adds to the antique effect.

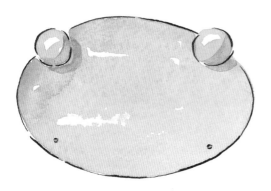

8 Drill four 7 mm (³⁄₈ in) diameter holes into the plywood base to fit the dowels, positioning two at each end of the oval shape, close to the edge. Glue the dowels into the holes, pushing them in until the ball is touching the plywood base.

9 Insert the wooden base into the recessed stand of the washtub. Then drill a few small holes through the base of the tub and the plywood stand to ensure good drainage.

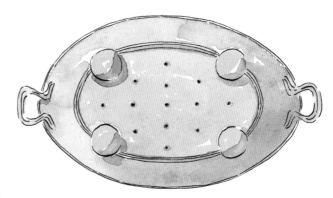

10 If your tub is a suitable colour, you may wish to leave it. However, both enamel and tin can be painted to suit a particular planting scheme. Gilding looks best against dark colours; navy-blue matt emulsion has been used here.

11 Fill the tub with compost to 130 mm (5 in) below the top, forming a slightly dome-shaped surface. Remove the tobacco plants from their pots and arrange them in the tub; for a colourful and dense mound of flowers, mix up the reds and pinks and position the root balls close together. Fill in the gaps with the remaining compost, firm in and keep well watered. Place the moss around the plants to help to retain moisture and for neatness.

alternative planting scheme
Place the tub indoors, in a kitchen or conservatory, or raise it on a plinth and plant with trailing ivy (*Hedera helix*).

patinated terracotta

Many modern terracotta pots, especially machine-made varieties, have a raw new look
that can detract from the effect of an attractive planting scheme. They can also look out
of place next to old containers that have softened with age. One answer is to tone down
new pots using special paint to simulate patinated terracotta. In this project we show
how to age a terracotta trough artificially by this method.

MATERIALS & EQUIPMENT

1 new terracotta trough 600 x 230 x 230 mm (24 x 9 x 9 in)

2 naturally patinated terracotta pots with 250 mm (10 in) diameter

small pot off-white or grey oil-bound distemper

small paintbrush

pot shards

20 litres loam-based compost

3 creeping soft grass (*Holcus mollis* 'Albovariegatus'),
in 150 mm (6 in) diameter pots

2 box balls (*Buxus sempervirens*)

1   Prepare the paint by putting a tablespoon of distemper into 300 ml (½ pint) of cold water and mixing well.

2   Coat the outside of the trough with this watered-down solution using a small-headed paintbrush. Make sure that you paint right into the curves and indents on the relief detail.

3   When the distemper is dry, scrub it off using a stiff brush dipped into a bucket of cold water. The object is to leave a white deposit in the relief detail and around the moulding edges, but to remove the paint from the flat surfaces almost entirely, except for the odd blemish. Don't worry about scrubbing off all the paint – what remains sinks into the pores of the terracotta, ensuring that a subtle colour variation remains. If necessary, apply another thin wash to the relief detail and scrub off again.

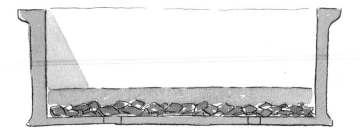

4   Fill the bottom of the trough to a depth of 20 mm (¾ in) with pot shards to help drainage. Cover this layer with enough loam-based compost to raise the top of the grass pots to 25 mm (1 in) below the top edge of the container.

5   Remove the grasses from their pots and place them on the compost layer, then fill the remaining space with compost, and firm down gently. Soak the compost and check often to make sure the soil has not dried out. After eight weeks or so apply a weak liquid fertilizer, and continue to feed on a monthly basis in spring, summer and autumn.

6 Plant up the two naturally patinated containers with the box balls, lining the bases with pot shards and filling with compost, as for the trough.

7 Display these pots on either side of the trough. The naturally aged appearance of the terracotta pots develops only after several years of outdoor use, but the artificially patinated trough that has been instantly aged sits well between them.

alternative effect
For a more heavily patinated look, create an antiqued bronze appearance. Although more complicated than the patinated effect, this is still easy to achieve.

1 Create a glaze by mixing one part water to one part deep blue-green matt emulsion. Wipe it over the outside of the trough with a rag.

2 Create two more glazes as before with pale blue and pale green matt emulsion and apply them in random strokes using a small paintbrush. Dip the brush in water and drag it around the rim, letting the water run down the trough in streaks. Allow to dry. Blend the glazes with fine-grade steel wool.

3 Finally, make a glaze with white matt emulsion and apply a thin coat to the surface of the trough; while the paint is still wet wipe it off with a damp cloth, leaving small deposits in the moulding and just enough to soften the blue and green colours.

painted pots

A good way of introducing vibrant colour to an ordinary terracotta pot is to paint it.
Paint also disguises the rather harsh-looking red appearance of so much machine-made
terracotta. Use the green and yellow scheme chosen here or pick your own combination to
match the architectural background of your garden. To create the greatest impact, paint
the pots in simple striking designs and pick plants to match the overall colour scheme.

MATERIALS & EQUIPMENT

6 machine-made terracotta pots: 2 with 230 mm (9 in) diameters,
2 with 170 mm (7 in) diameters, 2 with 150 mm (6 in) diameters

1 litre (1¾ pints) each yellow matt emulsion and palm-green matt emulsion

masking tape 25 mm (1 in) wide

paintbrush and watercolour brush

pot shards

30 litres general-purpose compost

10 lilies (*Lilium* 'Reinesse')

10 *Osteospermum* 'Buttermilk'

6 lime-and-cream petunias

1   Begin by painting one of each size of pot in green; coat the outside and the top 40 mm (1½ in) on the inside. Repeat for the remaining pots using the yellow paint; you may find that it takes two coats of yellow to hide the terracotta colouring beneath. Wait for the paint to dry before applying the pattern.

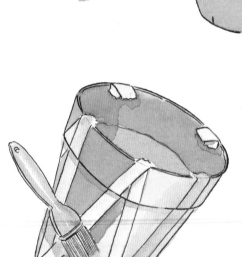

2   Use the largest pots for the zigzag design. Divide the circumference at the base into five equal parts and mark with a pencil. Then divide the top into five, placing these marks exactly midway between the ones already made around the base.

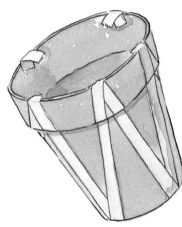

3   Apply the masking tape in strips, joining the top and bottom marks so that a zigzag pattern is formed on the outside of the pots.

4   On the outside, paint the green-based pot yellow, overlapping the edges of the masking tape, and paint the yellow-based pot green. Peel off the tape when the paint is completely dry to reveal a neat zigzag pattern.

5   Select another yellow pot and a green pot and decorate with 25 mm (1 in) diameter spots in the contrasting colour using a watercolour brush; draw freehand or make a template by cutting a circle out of a 100 mm (4 in) square of card and painting over it. Finish the pots by painting the top band in the same colour as the spots.

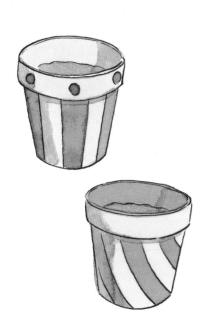

6 In this arrangement the other two pots have been left plain, but you can devise any pattern of your choice, remembering that simple bold designs work best. Here are some alternatives.

7 Use the larger pots for the lilies. 'Reinesse' is a stem-rooting lily, so line the pot with pot shards and plant 150–200 mm (6–8 in) deep to allow for root development. If you choose a basal-rooting lily, such as *Lilium candidum*, plant 100–150 mm (4–6 in) deep. Plant bulbs from autumn to spring, or pot-grown lilies any time. Fill in with compost, water and protect from frost.

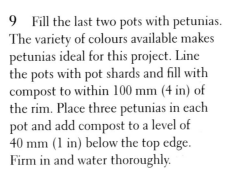

8 Line two more pots with pot shards and half-fill them with compost. Place five osteospermums in each and fill with compost. Bring these plants indoors in the autumn and winter to protect them from frost.

9 Fill the last two pots with petunias. The variety of colours available makes petunias ideal for this project. Line the pots with pot shards and fill with compost to within 100 mm (4 in) of the rim. Place three petunias in each pot and add compost to a level of 40 mm (1 in) below the top edge. Firm in and water thoroughly.

brickwork &
stone projects

a small brick-edged herb garden

This narrow herb border can be positioned against the wall of a house, preferably
a south-facing wall. It contains basic culinary herbs as well as a selection of scented
herbs. The angled brick edging is a simple way of providing a decorative divider
between the bed and the adjacent gravel path, a technique that was
particularly popular in the 19th century.

MATERIALS & EQUIPMENT

4 wooden pegs

5.7 m (19 ft) string

well-rotted manure

small bag cement

bag of soft sand

28 frost-resistant paving bricks

brick hardcore

gravel

hard clinker, rolled and rammed

pot-grown culinary herbs (see page 81)

builder's square • metal soil tamper • lump hammer

1   Choose a sunny location with good drainage, preferably against a south-facing wall. Measure out a plot 2000 x 850 mm (80 x 34 in) with pegs and string. Use a builder's square to check that the corners are right angles. Remove any turf with a spade and dig over the soil (see Double Digging, page 250).

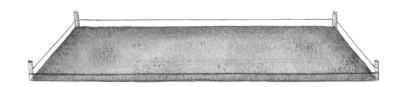

2   The bricks should be laid in the same direction at a 45° angle around three sides of the plot. Dig a trench around the three sides about 150 mm (6 in) deep and 130 mm (5 in) wide. Compact the earth in the trench – a metal soil tamper will do the job best.

3   Mix five parts soft sand to one part cement, make a well in the middle and add water to form a stiff cohesive paste. Fill the base of the trench about 65 mm (2½ in) deep and set the bricks into the cement bedding. The bricks do not have to be mortared together.

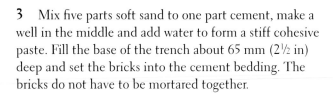

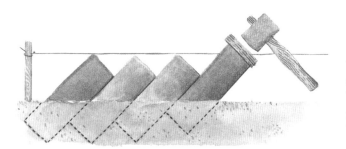

4   Level the edging by setting up a string 130 mm (5 in) above soil level, all the way around the brick-edged bed. Use the lump hammer to tamp down the bricks to the required level, first placing a piece of wood in between the brick and hammer to protect the side of the brick.

5   This bed has been edged by a gravel border. After the edging has set, lay the gravel on a bed of brick hardcore topped with the rolled and rammed hard clinker, as shown.

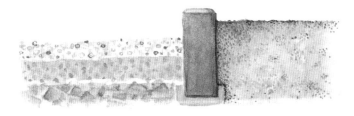

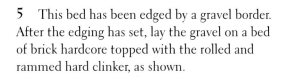

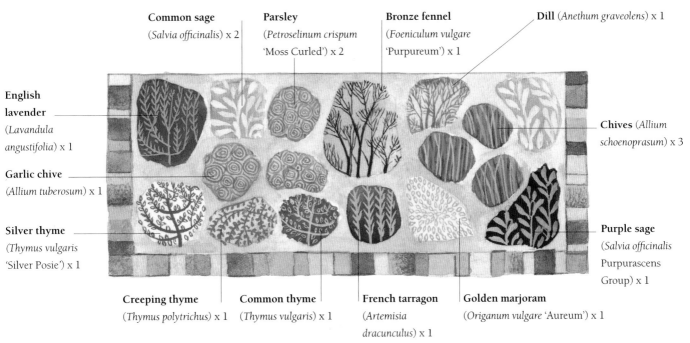

Common sage
(*Salvia officinalis*) x 2

Parsley
(*Petroselinum crispum*
'Moss Curled') x 2

Bronze fennel
(*Foeniculum vulgare*
'Purpureum') x 1

Dill (*Anethum graveolens*) x 1

**English
lavender**
(*Lavandula
angustifolia*) x 1

Garlic chive
(*Allium tuberosum*) x 1

Silver thyme
(*Thymus vulgaris*
'Silver Posie') x 1

Chives (*Allium
schoenoprasum*) x 3

Purple sage
(*Salvia officinalis*
Purpurascens
Group) x 1

Creeping thyme
(*Thymus polytrichus*) x 1

Common thyme
(*Thymus vulgaris*) x 1

French tarragon
(*Artemisia
dracunculus*) x 1

Golden marjoram
(*Origanum vulgare* 'Aureum') x 1

6 Buy pot-grown herbs for planting
in the autumn or spring and avoid frosty
weather. Plant the herbs according to
the scheme illustrated above.

a brickwork trough

A tall brick structure creates a stronger visual impact than could be achieved by an urn or a small planter. This trough provides the opportunity for a stunning display of flowering and non-flowering plants, which should nevertheless be simple enough to appreciate from a distance. The trough can be used for a mixture of permanent structural planting and seasonal bedding out – and will act as an important focal point in the garden all year round.

MATERIALS & EQUIPMENT

foundations: a small bag of cement, 50 kg (1 cwt) aggregate, 25 kg (½ cwt) sharp sand

mortar: a small bag of cement, 50 kg (1 cwt) soft sand

105 frost-resistant bricks (Old Cheshires have been used here)

1 piece exterior-grade plywood 450 x 450 x 10 mm (18 x 18 x ½ in)

4 concrete blocks 450 x 230 x 100 mm (18 x 9 x 4 in)

30 litres John Innes no. 2 potting compost

1 half-standard rose (*Rosa* 'Sanders' White Rambler')

4 *Hebe pinguifolia* 'Pagei'

18 tobacco plants (*Nicotiana alata* 'Lime Green')

pegs and string • spirit level

1 The trough needs to be built on foundations 130 mm (5 in) deep. Excavate an 825 mm (33 in) square hole to this depth. If your trough is to be sited on a gravel path, rake away the gravel from the area before digging your hole.

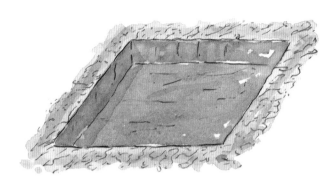

2 About two barrowloads of concrete are needed for the foundations. The ratio of the mix is six aggregate to three sharp sand and one cement. Mix these dry ingredients on a plywood board. Make a well in the centre and start to add water. Mix to form a stiff cohesive paste and transfer the concrete to a barrow.

3 Tip the concrete into the prepared hole, spreading it right into the corners. Level off with a straight-edged board and make sure there are no air pockets; use a spirit level to check that the surface is horizontal. Leave to dry out for at least 24 hours, and preferably several days, using a polythene sheet to protect it from the weather.

4 Mark out 680 mm (27 in) square with string and pegs, 65 mm (2½ in) above the concrete bed, to guide the first course of bricks.

5 Make the mortar as for the concrete (see step 2), using the ratio of four parts soft sand to one part cement. Spread a 10 mm (½ in) thick layer on the slab.

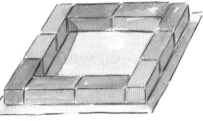

6 Position the bricks according to the plan. Lay the first course with the 'frog' at the top, butting all brick ends with mortar. Place the second layer staggered over the joints on the first. After this and each course, remove excess mortar from the joints, flush with the brick face, and point.

7 Continue to build the container until it has nine layers of brick; make sure that the face and height are even by checking at regular intervals with a spirit level.

8 Complete the trough with a coping course, stepping out the brick by 25 mm (1 in) to create a top moulding. Four filler pieces 100 x 50 mm (4 x 2 in) are needed to stretch the coping over the edges.

9 Fill the inside corners of the step with concrete to strengthen the join.

10 To avoid having to fill the entire container with compost, make a plywood stage. First drill five 25 mm (1 in) diameter holes in the wood for drainage. Then place the four concrete blocks inside the structure and rest the plywood over them.

11 For the following planting plan, the hebes and half-standard rose remain in their plastic pots but are set in soil, whereas the tobacco plants are de-potted and planted directly into the compost.

12 Position the rose in the centre, below the level of the top of the container, then fill with enough compost to sit the hebes flush with the coping layer. Finally, fill in the spaces with compost, placing the tobacco plants around the rose. Keep the display well watered and use a liquid feed weekly.

alternative planting schemes
For winter, plant a half-standard holly (*Ilex* x *meserveae* 'Blue Prince') with ivy (*Hedera helix* 'Erecta'); for autumn, a *Pittosporum tenuifolium* 'Purpureum' with cyclamen (*Cyclamen cilicium*); and for spring a box cone (*Buxus sempervirens*) with a hyacinth (*Hyacinthus orientalis* 'Delft Blue') border.

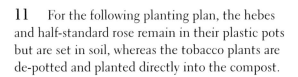

raised brick beds

Using raised beds in a vegetable garden is a very old tradition that has recently found favour again. The advantage over conventional beds is that there is an extra depth of good soil, allowing the plants to put their roots down in search of moisture and nutrition. The beds are designed in such a way that they can easily be reached from all sides so that there is no need to walk on and compact the soil – a big advantage.

MATERIALS & EQUIPMENT

hardcore

concrete

bricks

good loam

garden line or pegs and string

tamper

well-rotted organic material

seed and plants in variety

builder's trowel • spirit level

Please note: The raised brick beds are slightly more complex than other projects in this book. Unless you have previous experience of working with brick and stone, it is a good idea to consult a professional, using these plans as a guide.

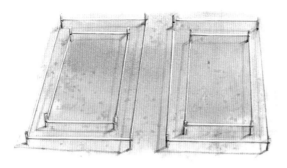

1 Think carefully about the construction of the beds. They should be just wide enough so that the centre can be reached from either side, and there should be adequate space to move between them. They should be in a sunny but sheltered position.

2 Dig two trenches forming rectangles 150 mm (6 in) longer and wider than the proposed beds. They should be 250 mm (10 in) wide and 400 mm (16 in) deep. Ram down 130 mm (5 in) of hardcore in the base and then pour and level 100 mm (4 in) of concrete on top of this.

3 The walls of the beds are brick; they are easy to construct and look attractive, but they could equally be made of concrete blocks, which are quicker to lay. Build up the walls so that there are two courses below ground and four above – about 300 mm (12 in) higher than the surrounding soil. See step 4.

4 Once the soil in the bed has been dug, water should drain away easily. But to ensure that no water gets trapped within the walls, a vertical joint should be left uncemented every 450 mm (18 in) when laying the course of bricks at ground level.

5 When the cement has hardened, prepare the bed. Kill or remove all traces of perennial weeds. Dig the soil to at least one spade depth but preferably double dig it to two, being careful not to bring any subsoil into the top layer. Add plenty of organic material.

6 Once the existing soil in the beds has been cleaned and dug, add a mixture of good-quality topsoil (loam) and well-rotted organic material. Fill the beds right up. Do this in autumn and leave over winter for it to weather. Top up with more soil and compost in spring.

7 The area between the beds needs to be kept clear for easy access. To prevent it becoming a mass of weeds or a muddy track, it can be covered with paving slabs.

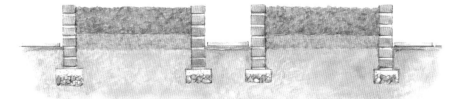

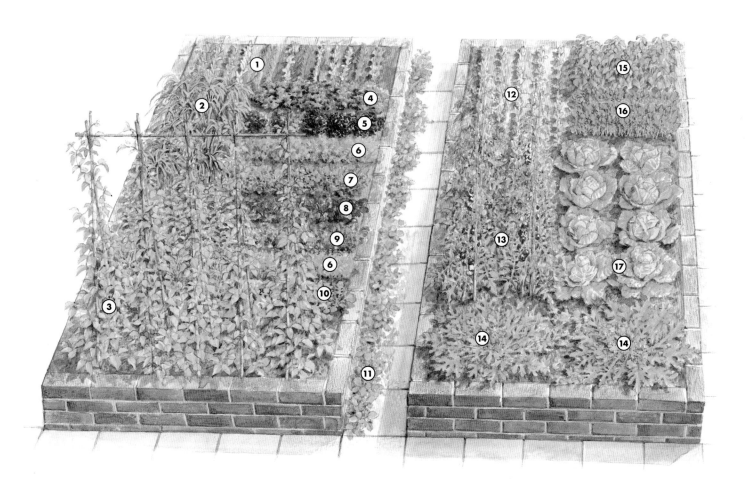

8 Plant the vegetables in blocks or rows. If you cannot reach directly into the centre of the beds, lay a plank between the rows to walk upon. Left in position, planks will also help keep the weeds down and retain moisture.

planting scheme

1 Seeds	**6** Carrots	**11** Alpine	**15** Dwarf beans
2 Leeks	**7** Turnips	strawberries	**16** Celery
3 Runner beans	**8** Beetroot	**12** Lettuce	**17** Cabbages
4 Parsley	**9** Parsnips	**13** Tomatoes	
5 Lettuce	**10** Swedes	**14** Courgettes	

a raised flower bed

In small paved gardens there seems to be little choice but to grow plants in pots.
However, for a larger display, a generous raised bed is ideal as it will hold sufficient
soil to sustain a number of plants, both perennials and annuals. Raised beds
also create different levels, which add interest to the space. If they border
a path, the extra height can be used to display angular and trailing foliage.

MATERIALS & EQUIPMENT

hardcore • concrete • crocks or stones

grass turves or a sheet of horticultural polythene

bricks, stone, concrete blocks, timbers or
railway sleepers (no foundations needed for wood)

1 *Corylus maxima* 'Purpurea'

4 *Phormium tenax* 'Purpureum'

8 *Heuchera micrantha* var. *diversifolia* 'Palace Purple'

*Please note: The raised flower bed is slightly more complex than other projects in this book.
Unless you have previous experience of working with brick and stone, it is a good idea
to consult a professional, using these plans as a guide.*

1 A paved garden, with its strong architectural identity, lends itself to symmetrical, well-blended displays and plants with bold foliage forms. Plan the raised bed accordingly, using plants that will stand up to scrutiny as people walk along the path: full foliage and fragrance are assets. This large raised bed is 3.6 x 2.5 m (12 x 8 ft).

2 Choose a material for building your raised bed: brick, as here, stone, concrete blocks and wood are all possibilities. Wood is perhaps the easiest to use, especially if old railway sleepers can be found; these are heavy baulks of timber that make sturdy walls. They are longer-lasting than other forms of wood as they have been impregnated with tar, but therein lies their drawback: in hot conditions they ooze tar.

3 Brick, stone and concrete blocks are used in the same way. If a brick bed is not to be built on a solid base, dig foundations to a depth of about 250 mm (10 in). Ram a 100 mm (4 in) layer of hardcore into this, topped by a 150 mm (6 in) layer of concrete. Build the wall on top.

4 Drainage holes should be left in the lower levels of the brickwork to allow excess water to drain away. A few gaps in the vertical pointing are usually sufficient.

5 For brick walls, a line of tiles can be added towards the top. This detail is not essential, but partly decorative and partly to direct water away from the wall, so that the surface is not stained by repeated drenchings.

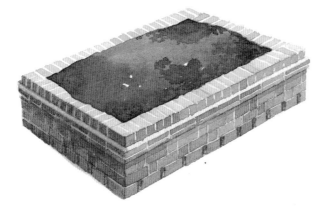

6 To aid drainage, add broken crocks or stones to a depth of 70 mm (3 in) or more, then a layer of upturned turves (shown above) or horticultural polythene with drainage holes. Fill with good-quality loam with plenty of well-rotted organic matter and some grit to help drainage (left). Firm down as you go and overfill, as the soil will sink with time.

7 Plant the bed with flowering plants according to the scheme shown at right, or devise your own scheme. Once filled with soil, raised beds can be treated like any other border, with the full range of plants that that implies. They allow great scope for the garden designer, but it is essential to plan and build these structures carefully if they are to work well.

planting scheme
1 *Corylus maxima* 'Purpurea' x 1
2 *Phormium tenax* 'Purpureum' x 4
3 *Heuchera micrantha* var. *diversifolia* 'Palace Purple' x 8

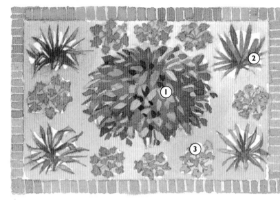

8 Keep the soil in raised beds topped up and check that the structure is draining efficiently.

alternative materials
Railway sleepers are laid directly onto a flat base. When using them, stagger the vertical joins, as with brickwork, to give a firmer finish. Leave small gaps for drainage. Remember to lift the timbers with care as they are heavy.

Slabs of light brown and grey stones give quite a different finish to a wall of bricks. They are particularly well suited to cottages and country houses and, if the house is of stone, ideally the same local material should be used.

a herb-lined pathway

A brick or paved pathway makes a herb garden accessible even in wet or muddy weather. Paths also define a design, fulfilling much the same role as dwarf hedges or grass edging. You do not need much space to make this type of pathway; the herb bed in this project will fit even the tiniest of town gardens. Leave the paving to set and dry for a few days before planting. Allow the herbs to flow informally over the edges of the path.

MATERIALS & EQUIPMENT

4 wooden pegs

7 m (23 ft) string

well-rotted manure

1 paving slab 600 x 600 mm (2 x 2 ft)

9 frost-resistant paving bricks

bag of sharp sand

small bag of cement

5 plastic pots or buckets

1 terracotta plant pot 300 mm (12 in) in diameter

pot-grown herbs (see page 97)

builder's square • edging spade

soil tamper (optional) • spirit level

1 Dig out your bed ready for an autumn or a spring planting, choosing a partly shaded location. Mark out a 1.5 x 1.8 m (5 x 6 ft) plot with wooden pegs and string, using a builder's square to check that the corners are right angles. Remove the turf with an edging spade and dig over the soil (see Double Digging, page 250).

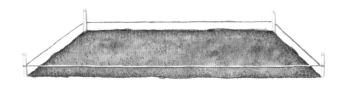

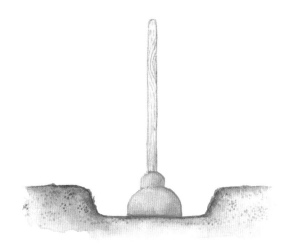

2 The bricks used here are high-fired engineering bricks (although any paving brick is suitable); their purplish colour works well with the purple sage in the planting. To lay the brick paving and slab, dig out a trench 250 mm (10 in) wide to a depth of 150 mm (6 in). Make a 600 mm (24 in) square for the paving slab. (See opposite for path and slab layout.) Compress the soil in the trench with a soil tamper or use your feet to provide a solid base for the concrete and paving.

3 Prepare a mortar mix of five parts sharp sand to one part cement. Lay a bed of mortar in the ditch to a depth of 90 mm (3½ in) and set the bricks and paving slab into the mortar bed. You do not need to mortar between each brick. Gently tap down the bricks and use the spirit level to check that they are level as you go.

4 Allow the paving to set and dry thoroughly for a few days before planting the herbs in the bed. Before starting to plant, incorporate some gravel where you plant the thyme, if your soil is not free-draining.

5 Buy good-sized herbs that have been grown in 100 mm (4 in) diameter pots; the summer savory and bay can be bought in 150 mm (6 in) diameter pots. Plant the herbs in autumn or spring according to the planting scheme. Plant the mints in buckets or pots and then sink them into the ground, because mint can be invasive. Plant the golden lemon balm in a 300 mm (12 in) diameter clay pot to provide a focal point in the centre of the bed.

Variegated gingermint
(*Mentha* x *gracilis* 'Variegata') x 3

Wild strawberry
(*Fragaria vesca*) x 2

Golden lemon balm
(*Melissa officinalis* 'Aurea') x 1

Bay
(*Laurus nobilis*) x 1

Golden marjoram
(*Origanum vulgare* 'Aureum') x 2

Variegated gingermint
(*Mentha* x *gracilis* 'Variegata') x 2

Lemon thyme
(*Thymus* x *citriodorus*
'Bertram Anderson') x 4

Wild strawberry
(*Fragaria vesca*) x 2

Summer savory
(*Satureja hortensis*) x 1

Golden marjoram
(*Origanum vulgare* 'Aureum') x 2

Oregano
(*Origanum vulgare*) x 2

Bay
(*Laurus nobilis*) x 1

Summer savory
(*Satureja hortensis*) x 1

Purple sage
(*Salvia officinalis*
Purpurascens Group) x 3

Lemon thyme
(*Thymus* x *citriodorus*
'Bertram Anderson') x 4

6 Trim back the herbs when necessary to prevent them swamping each other. Cut back new growth on the bay in early summer. Cut back the sage before it flowers to achieve a compact shape. Trim the thyme after flowering to encourage bushy growth.

a retaining wall

Slopes in a garden can present problems. One solution is to make a virtue of them by dividing the garden into different levels using retaining walls. These can be planted up in any number of ways, from grass to highly ornamental displays, and so help to define different parts of the garden. The surface of the wall can also become a decorative feature in its own right, weathering over time with trailing plants growing in nooks and crannies.

MATERIALS & EQUIPMENT

for every 2.5 m (8 ft) of wall

0.2 cu m (6 cu ft) concrete

½ bag cement

2 bags soft sand

0.2 cu m (6 cu ft) of random-sized stone blocks (approximately 20)

2 terracotta drainage pipes

for the bed

0.1 cu m (4 cu ft) of rubble or hardcore

0.1 cu m (4 cu ft) good topsoil or 2 bags well-rotted organic material

bricklaying trowel • wheelbarrow

*Please note: The retaining wall is slightly more complex than other projects in this book.
Unless you have previous experience of working with brick and stone, it is a good idea
to consult a professional, using these plans as a guide.*

1 There are several ways of using a retaining wall on a sloping site. The position of the wall will depend on how you want to redefine the area, minimizing the difference in levels (above left) or making a stepped finish (below left). Any form of walling can be used: brick, stone or concrete blocks. A wall that is higher than 450 mm (18 in) should be built by a professional.

2 The finished wall will be 300 mm (12 in) high; like all brick and stone walls, it must have foundations. If the wall is to support an existing bank, as here, dig away some of the bank to allow you to work. Dig a trench 200 mm (8 in) deep along the line of the wall, three times as wide as the final wall will be. Add a 150 mm (6 in) layer of concrete.

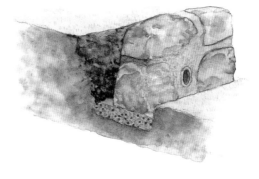

3 Start building the wall. Just above ground level, insert a short length of pipe and secure it in place so that it is in line with the visible base. This will allow water to seep away and is very important to prevent the bed becoming waterlogged. Add a pipe every 1 m (3 ft). Alternatively, leave spaces between the stones to facilitate drainage.

4 Build above the pipe until the required height is reached. If you plan to include trailing plants in the wall itself, leave a few gaps in the cement for planting.

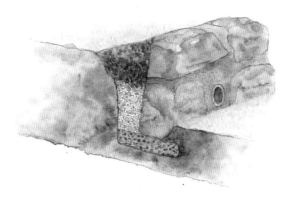

5 To aid drainage, place a layer of rubble or hardcore between the bed and the wall. Backfill with soil rich in organic matter. If you use the soil that was removed from the bank, avoid putting subsoil near the surface.

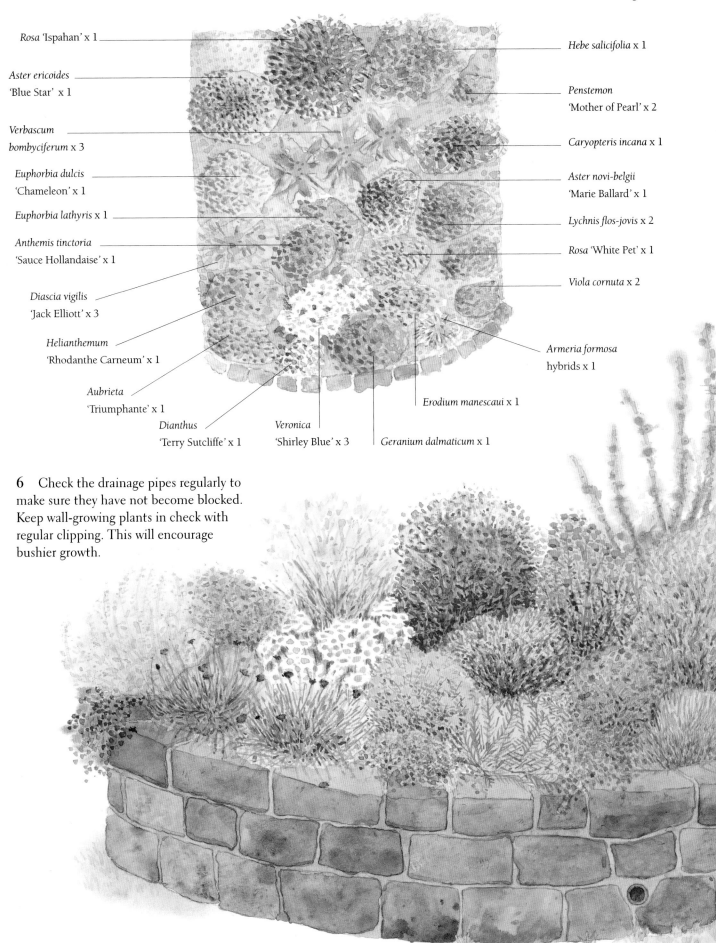

Rosa 'Ispahan' x 1

Aster ericoides
'Blue Star' x 1

*Verbascum
bombyciferum* x 3

Euphorbia dulcis
'Chameleon' x 1

Euphorbia lathyris x 1

Anthemis tinctoria
'Sauce Hollandaise' x 1

Diascia vigilis
'Jack Elliott' x 3

Helianthemum
'Rhodanthe Carneum' x 1

Aubrieta
'Triumphante' x 1

Dianthus
'Terry Sutcliffe' x 1

Veronica
'Shirley Blue' x 3

Geranium dalmaticum x 1

Erodium manescaui x 1

Hebe salicifolia x 1

Penstemon
'Mother of Pearl' x 2

Caryopteris incana x 1

Aster novi-belgii
'Marie Ballard' x 1

Lychnis flos-jovis x 2

Rosa 'White Pet' x 1

Viola cornuta x 2

Armeria formosa
hybrids x 1

6 Check the drainage pipes regularly to make sure they have not become blocked. Keep wall-growing plants in check with regular clipping. This will encourage bushier growth.

101

a wall cascade

Walls can make a very positive contribution to garden design, especially in a small garden, where every inch of space should be used effectively. Decorate them with plants, plaques, containers or a water feature, which can range from a simple spout to a cascade and pond. The slate 'steps' pictured right have been drilled with outlet holes, but a simple hollow, as used in the project, is just as effective. Double-check all measurements in advance.

MATERIALS & EQUIPMENT

foundations

hardcore (multiply the size of the pond by 150 mm (6 in) for the cubic volume of hardcore required)

two 25 kg (55 lb) bags concrete

1800 x 600 mm (6 x 2 ft) sheet reinforcing mesh

ten 25 kg (55 lb) bags aggregate

walls

5 slabs of slate or cast concrete, 690 x 400 x 60 mm (27 x 16 x 2½ in), slightly dished

enough bricks to build the pond edge and wall to the required dimensions

five 25 kg (55 lb) bags cement

twenty 25 kg (55 lb) bags soft sand

sixteen 250 x 300 mm (10 x 12 in) capping slabs

pond

one 1.5 x 2.7 m (5 x 9 ft) butyl or welded rubber pond liner

two 1.5 x 2.7 m (5 x 9 ft) sheets garden fleece

low-volume submersible pump with its fittings

2.2 m (7 ft) length of 10 mm (½ in) alkathene water pipe

bricklayer's trowel ● club hammer

bolster ● spirit level ● bricklaying line

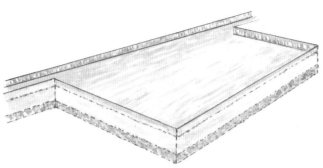

1   Start by laying the foundations. Dig out the area covered by the walls and pool to a depth of 530 mm (21 in). Fill with 150 mm (6 in) of hardcore, rubble or broken stones and ram this down. Cover with 300 mm (12 in) of concrete – do not fill to ground level – burying a sheet of reinforcing mesh in the middle of the layer.

2   Build all the walls two bricks wide. Embed the pipe in the back wall, creating a space by knocking off the inner corners of the bricks along the line of the pipe. The pipe should run from 100 mm (4 in) above the top of the concrete foundations to the point where the water emerges from the wall onto the top slab. When you reach the required height of the pond, stop building, line the pond with garden fleece and then seal it with a pond liner.

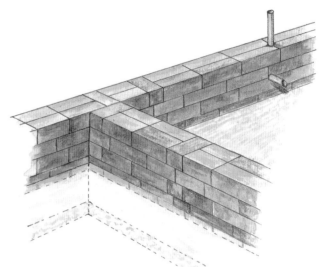

3   Cover the contours of the pond with the liner, leaving 80 mm (3 in) to overlap onto the pond wall. Secure the liner into the back wall with capping slabs.

4   Continue to build the back wall and add the slabs at appropriate intervals. Cement them into the wall to a depth of one row of bricks (below right). The slabs should be slightly dished, carved out by a stonemason if slate is used, or cast into the concrete. Raise one end of each slab by about 5 mm (¼ in) to allow the water to run off the other end (above right).

5 Secure the top slab in the back wall just below the end of the pipe so that the water flows directly onto it. Top the pond wall with capping slabs; these form a decorative finish, provide a surface for plants or for sitting and, above all, hold the pond liner in place.

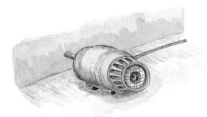

6 Install a submersible pump by following the instructions supplied with the unit. Connect it to the lower end of the pipe where it emerges into the pool and run the waterproof cable out over one corner at the back of the pool. Hide the cable under plants.

Please note: Always employ a professional bricklayer to build tall walls if you lack experience and an electrician to install the pump if you have any doubts.

7 Check regularly that the pump is working effectively, the pipe is clear of debris and the pond liner is intact and secure.

wood & metal
garden structures

a trellis screen

Freestanding trellis is an absolute boon for the gardener. It allows instant screening from the outside world and is ideal for the creation of 'rooms' within the garden. Trellis is perfect for supporting climbing plants in their numerous forms, creating a dense screen of foliage and colour. This versatile garden structure can also be incorporated into arches, pergolas or arbours, providing a foothold for plants while allowing light and air through.

MATERIALS & EQUIPMENT

trellis panels

100 x 100 mm (4 x 4 in) posts, each one 300 mm (12 in) taller than the trellis panels

1 finial per post

½ bucket broken rocks per hole

3 buckets dry-mix concrete per hole

100 mm (4 in) galvanized nails

clematis, roses, honeysuckle or other climbing plants

plant ties

spirit level

1   Freestanding trellis must be bedded in firmly. Set posts so that one third of their length is in the ground. So, a 1.2 m (4 ft) high trellis requires a hole that is 600 mm (2 ft) deep, plus 150 mm (6 in) for a layer of hardcore. For the first post, dig a suitable hole and add a 150 mm (6 in) layer of broken rocks. Put the post in the hole, ensuring it is upright, and pack dry-mix concrete around it. Cover with soil.

2   Once the main post is solidly in place, nail the first trellis panel to the post using long galvanized nails. Support the far end of the panel at the same time. Align the next post to ensure a neat fit for the trellis and dig the foundation hole.

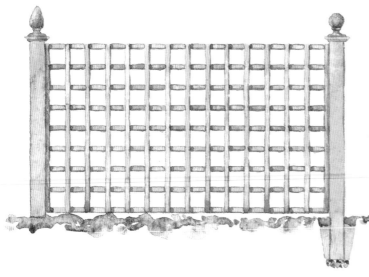

3   Add the hardcore base and secure the second post in its hole with concrete. Ensuring that both are upright and square, nail the panel to the post.

4   If you are adding more panels, repeat the process. Once the screen is complete, plant the bed in front.

alternative finials and finishes
Finials are available in different designs, from round to pyramid- and spear-shaped. They can make a remarkable difference to the finished effect and are simple to fix in place. Trellis can be left as natural wood, painted traditional white or stained subtle colours such as bluish-green.

5   If using clematis, see page 258 for pruning and training. The varieties used here – *Clematis* 'Perle d'Azur and *C. texensis* – are both group 3 plants, which should be cut right back to just above a strong pair of buds in early spring. After pruning, check that the trellis is secure and treat with plant-friendly preservative.

a rustic trellis

The wood used for this trellis has not been machined, making it pleasingly irregular in thickness and shape. The structure can be covered with plants, but rustic trellis is attractive in its own right if a more restrained covering is preferred. The trellis is available ready-made but it is simple to make – it does not require advanced carpentry skills – and making your own allows you to tailor the design to your exact needs.

MATERIALS & EQUIPMENT

foundations

½ bucket hardcore per hole

3 buckets concrete per hole

spirit level

for each 1.8 m (6 ft) section of trellis

2 poles for uprights, 2.5 m (8 ft) long and 100–125 mm (4–5 in) across, for the first section and then 1 per section

2 poles for crossbars, 2.5 m (8 ft) long and 80–100 mm (3–4 in) across

3 poles for struts, 900 mm (3 ft) long and 80–100 mm (3–4 in) across

100 mm (4 in) galvanized nails

wood preservative

plants in variety (see page 115)

1 Secure the upright posts (see page 110), first stripping the bark from the section that is to be held in the ground and treating it with preservative. Once the posts are firm, attach the crossbars using simple halved joints (where half the thickness is removed) and long galvanized nails.

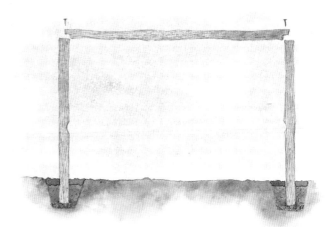

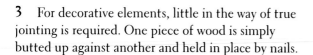

2 The most important joints are those where the crossbars meet the main upright posts. A simple niche can be cut into the post to correspond with the pointed end of each crossbar. Do not cut too far into the post as this will weaken it. Secure the wood with long nails.

3 For decorative elements, little in the way of true jointing is required. One piece of wood is simply butted up against another and held in place by nails.

4 The diagonal bars are useful for training climbers. Measure the bars carefully, make right-angled ends and secure them into the framework with nails.

planting scheme

Plants suitable for climbing over rustic trellising include clematis, climbing and rambling roses, honeysuckle and grape vines. The trellis needs to look balanced so complementary plants should be selected to grow beneath the structure. The scheme below measures 1.8 x 1.2 m (6 x 4 ft).

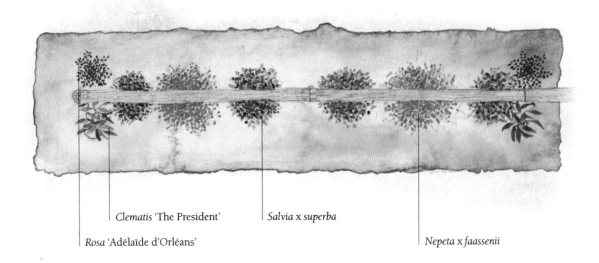

Clematis 'The President' *Salvia* x *superba*

Rosa 'Adélaïde d'Orléans' *Nepeta* x *faassenii*

5 If the whole trellis is treated with preservative (not just the areas of the main posts that are sunk into the ground), the life of the structure will be extended. Do not use creosote as this can harm plants. In early spring check that the trellis is secure and replace any decayed parts.

6 The clematis is a group 2 plant (see page 258), so it should be pruned lightly in early spring. Do not prune the rose in the first year. After that, each year remove two or three whole stems after flowering; cut back the remaining stems by a quarter and reduce the side shoots by two-thirds.

a trellis-enclosed
herb garden

The effect of the planting in this enclosed garden is informal, with the herbs growing together to form solid mounds contained by more formal box and lavender edging and trellis fences. The garden is composed of four beds with repeat planting in opposite beds.

MATERIALS & EQUIPMENT

16 wooden pegs • 33.5 m (110 ft) string

bonemeal or root fertilizer and well-rotted manure

4 trellis corner units (see page 247)

16 concrete edging slabs 900 x 150 mm (36 x 6 in)

4 wooden obelisks (optional)

14 common box (*Buxus sempervirens*)

14 silver box (*B. sempervirens* 'Elegantissima')

4 pot-grown common box pyramids (*B. sempervirens*)

20 English lavender (*Lavandula angustifolia*)

2 pot-grown standard *Phillyrea angustifolia*

2 pot-grown standard honeysuckle (*Lonicera periclymenum*)

gravel

pot-grown culinary herbs (see page 119)

builder's square • edging spade

1 Using pegs and string, mark out a plot 4.5 x 4.5 m (15 x 15 ft). Use a builder's square to ensure that the corners are right angles. Remove the turf with an edging spade and dig over the soil (see Double Digging, page 250). Divide the plot into four beds 1.8 m (6 ft) square with 900 mm (3 ft) between each bed.

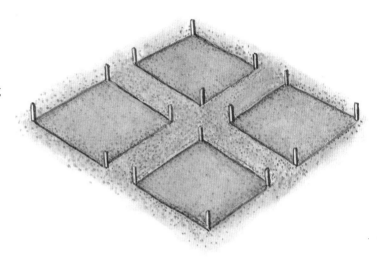

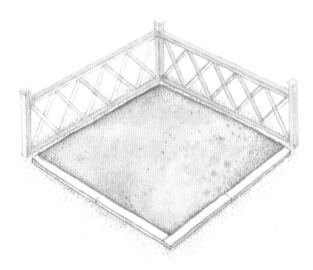

2 Enclose the beds with trellis corner units supported by posts sunk into metal holders. (Instructions for making the units are given on page 247. A total of 12 post and 12 post holders will be needed to make four units.) Edge the beds with concrete slabs sunk into the ground so that 50 mm (2 in) of the slabs show above soil level. Infill the paths between the beds with gravel to allow for easy access to the herbs.

3 Plant seven common box in each bed A, one every 230 mm (9 in), and five lavender, one every 260 mm (10¼ in), as shown. Bed B contains seven silver box and five lavender. Plant a box pyramid in each bed, one standard *Phillyrea angustifolia* in each bed A and one honeysuckle in each bed B. Place the obelisks, if using, according to the illustrations on page 119.

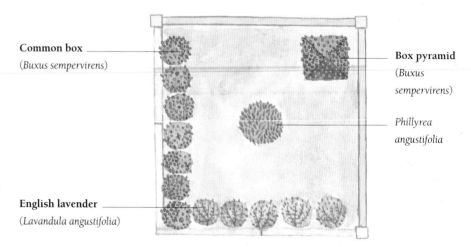

Common box
(*Buxus sempervirens*)

Box pyramid
(*Buxus sempervirens*)

Phillyrea angustifolia

English lavender
(*Lavandula angustifolia*)

4 Buy pot-grown herbs, preferably in 130 mm (5 in) pots. Plant them in late autumn or early spring according to the planting schemes for beds A and B shown on page 119 and repeat for the beds diagonally opposite.

5 Cut back the sage, tarragon and mint in late autumn. Trim the rosemary and lavender in mid-spring.

planting scheme for bed A

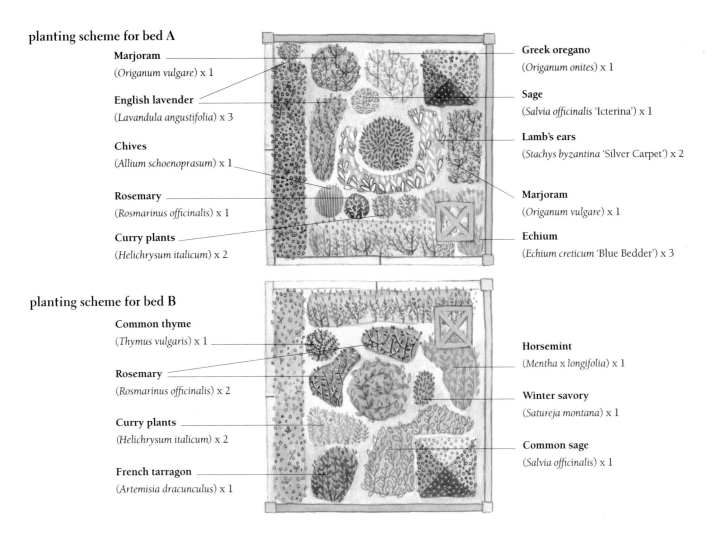

Marjoram
(*Origanum vulgare*) x 1

English lavender
(*Lavandula angustifolia*) x 3

Chives
(*Allium schoenoprasum*) x 1

Rosemary
(*Rosmarinus officinalis*) x 1

Curry plants
(*Helichrysum italicum*) x 2

Greek oregano
(*Origanum onites*) x 1

Sage
(*Salvia officinalis* 'Icterina') x 1

Lamb's ears
(*Stachys byzantina* 'Silver Carpet') x 2

Marjoram
(*Origanum vulgare*) x 1

Echium
(*Echium creticum* 'Blue Bedder') x 3

planting scheme for bed B

Common thyme
(*Thymus vulgaris*) x 1

Rosemary
(*Rosmarinus officinalis*) x 2

Curry plants
(*Helichrysum italicum*) x 2

French tarragon
(*Artemisia dracunculus*) x 1

Horsemint
(*Mentha* x *longifolia*) x 1

Winter savory
(*Satureja montana*) x 1

Common sage
(*Salvia officinalis*) x 1

vertical planting

A good way to secure privacy in a town gardens is to plant upwards. An ordinary hedge is a popular solution, but even on a roof terrace one can achieve more interesting screening effects using containers. This project shows how to get a banded effect of pleached lime underplanted with ivy, below which are containers for flowers. If you wish to enclose all sides of your garden, simply add more troughs and trellis backing.

MATERIALS & EQUIPMENT

2 concrete troughs 600 x 450 x 450 mm (24 x 18 x 18 in)

1 concrete trough 450 x 450 x 450 mm (18 x 18 x 18 in)

dark green matt emulsion

section of trellis 1.8 x 1.8 m (6 x 6 ft)

2 vertical wooden posts 2200 x 50 x 50 mm (84 x 2 x 2 in)

coated wire or garden ties

sea-washed pebbles

pot shards • soil-based compost and slow-release fertilizer

1 red-twigged lime (*Tilia platyphyllos* 'Rubra')

6 ivies (*Hedera helix*)

8 white petunias

8 purple *Verbena tenera*

8 white trailing *Verbena tenuisecta* f. *alba*

2 ferns (*Athyrium filix-femina*)

1 Start by securing the trellis. In this project vertical posts have been attached to the outside of a 300 mm (12 in) high parapet. If you don't have a wall, secure the posts in the ground. Space them 1.8 m (6 ft) apart so the trellis fits between them. Screw the trellis to the face of the posts 300 mm (12 in) above ground level. Or, if you have a high wall or wooden fence, you can train your plants along wires. Stretch plastic or galvanized wire horizontally between vine eyes at intervals and secure with screws.

2 Improve the appearance of the concrete troughs by coating them in matt emulsion. Dark colours work best with this planting scheme.

3 Plant the lime in the small trough. Choose a pot-grown specimen with a dense root system and a straight stem, ideally about 1.8 m (6 ft) high with lateral branches at the top; plant in autumn or early spring.

4 Cover the drainage holes of your container with pot shards and line with compost. Ease the lime out of its pot and position it towards the back of the trough. Plant the ferns in front of the lime and work compost around the root balls, making sure that they are level, and fill in with compost to within 80 mm (3 in) of the top. Add a top dressing of slow-release fertilizer and decorate the surface with pebbles.

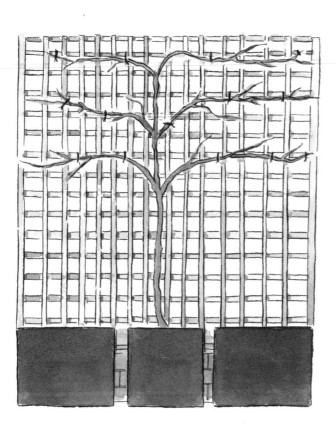

5 To achieve the striped effect at the top of the trellis, three lines of lateral branches have been trained horizontally. Start by choosing two strong laterals about 1.2 m (4 ft) from the base of the lime, on opposite sides of the stem. Secure them horizontally along the trellis with coated wire. Repeat for the next two lines, spacing them about 300 mm (12 in) apart.

6 Remove all the other side shoots from the stem and grow the trained laterals to the full width of the trellis. Prune annually and cut back excess foliage.

7   Next plant the two larger troughs on each side of the lime. Line the containers with pot shards and fill with compost to within 80 mm (3 in) of the top. Choose a plain green ivy with multiple stems that will provide a good hedge-like effect. Position three ivies at the back of each trough and top up with compost. If you want to create a dense screen, you can train the ivy into a fan shape, tying it to the trellis with coated wire.

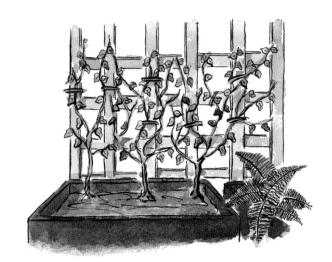

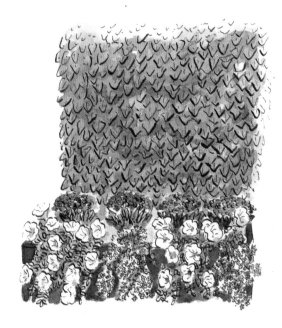

8   Grow the ivy to a height of 900 mm (3 ft) and allow the plants in both troughs to join together. Clip the ivy back to keep it flat against the trellis and maintain a straight line along the top; you don't want the ivy to meet the lime, since this would make the banded effect less well defined.

9   Complete the large troughs with a seasonal planting scheme. White petunias, purple verbenas and white trailing verbenas have been planted along the front to give a long summer show. Keep them well watered and fed. To make a longer wall screen or enclose a space, add to the number of troughs and secure extra panels of trellis.

alternative planting schemes
Plant forget-me-nots (*Myosotis alpestris*) for a blue haze in spring, or, for autumn, plant a pot-grown cylamen such as *Cyclamen cilicium* or *C. hederifolium*.

a scented arbour

An arbour is the perfect place to sit and relax, especially after a day's work. The scent of the climbers that clothe the arbour and the nature of the structure itself combine to soothing effect. The arbour's leafy and flowery walls create a sense of safe enclosure without being boxed in; it is open and closed at the same time. Here a simple structure is covered with 'New Dawn', a repeat-flowering rose that produces blooms all summer long.

MATERIALS & EQUIPMENT

2 wooden trellis panels 1.8 m x 900 mm (6 x 3 ft) for the sides

1 wooden trellis panel 2.5 x 1.8 m (8 x 6 ft) for the back

1 wooden trellis panel 2.5 m x 900 mm (8 x 3 ft) for the roof

4 square wooden posts 2.5 m x 100 mm x 100 mm (8 ft x 4 in x 4 in)

4 wooden finials

galvanized nails

2 buckets rubble or broken stones

0.25 cu m (8 cu ft) concrete

plant ties

rustic bench

2 *Rosa* 'New Dawn'

2 buckets compost

spirit level

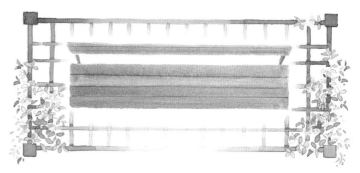

1   When buying the framework, allow ample space for table and chairs (if you plan to eat in the arbour) and for the spread of the rose, which will protrude at least 450 mm (18 in) into the seating area. Wooden or metal arbour frameworks are also available ready-made in a variety of shapes and sizes.

2   If the arbour is in a sheltered place, the posts can simply be buried in the ground 600 mm (24 in) deep and the earth rammed around them. For a more secure structure in an exposed position, the posts should be concreted in. Dig holes 600 mm (24 in) deep and place 100 mm (4 in) of rubble in the bottom. Insert the posts and use a spirit level to check that they are upright. Fill in the holes with concrete.

3   Fix the side and back trellis panels to the posts with galvanized nails. To prevent the wood splitting, drill pilot holes in the panels. An alternative is to use proprietary clips that are first nailed or screwed to the uprights and then to the panels. Make certain that the panels are level by using a spirit level. Nail or screw the decorative finials to the four posts.

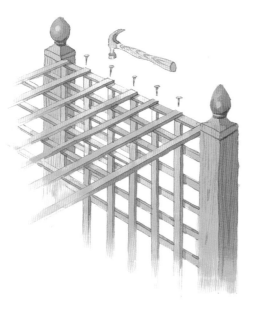

4   Cut the roof panel so that it rests on both the side and back trellis panels. Nail or screw the roof directly to the side panels, drilling pilot holes first. If the top rails of the side panels are not strong enough to hold the weight of the roof, reinforce them with 50 x 25 mm (2 x 1 in) wooden battens along their length.

5 Plant two roses, one at each of the back corners of the arbour. Prepare the ground by incorporating plenty of well-rotted organic material into the soil around the planting area. Dig a hole slightly wider than the root ball of the rose and then plant the rose so that the top of the root ball is level with top of the hole. Fill in with soil. Firm down the earth around the roots and water well. Place the bench in the arbour.

6 Spread the stems of the newly planted roses so that they fan out along the sides and back of the arbour. Tie in each shoot with a plant tie or string. As the shoots grow, continue to tie them in and arrange so that they eventually cover the whole arbour.

7 Like most climbing or rambling roses, *Rosa* 'New Dawn' is a vigorous plant that produces a profusion of blooms from midsummer to autumn. It can even be grown successfully in part-shaded sites.

a wooden obelisk

Trellis obelisks have long been used as a decorative element in the garden. They create an attractive feature on their own, or in pairs frame a view or emphasize a formal approach to a house. The shape of the obelisk makes it suitable for supporting climbers such as ivy, clematis, honeysuckle and hops. This project uses quick-growing hawthorn; as the hawthorn spreads, use the trellis as a clipping guide to create a tall, elegant pyramid shape.

MATERIALS & EQUIPMENT

sawn timber (see steps 1, 2, 5 and 6 on page 130)

square of exterior-grade plywood 380 x 380 x 10 mm (15 x 15 x ½ in)

no. 8 screws 40 mm (1½ in) and 50 mm (2 in)

sherardized panel pins 40 mm (1½ in)

1 litre (1¾ pints) clear wood preservative

1 litre (1¾ pints) wood stain

50 litres potting compost

pot shards

4 bare-root hawthorns (*Crataegeus monogyna*)

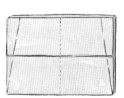

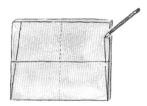

1 For each of the two short and two long sides of the tub, put together two 150 mm (6 in) wide timber boards. For the short sides, measure and mark the bottom length of 390 mm (15 in), draw a vertical line through its centre, then measure out the top length of 340 mm (13½ in) extending equally on each side of this line. Use these marks to draw the tapered sides before cutting out. Repeat for the two longer sides, measuring 430 mm (17 in) along the bottom and 380 mm (15 in) along the top.

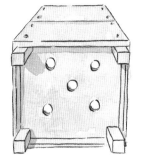

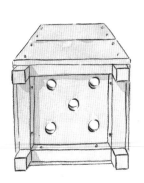

2 Take the two shorter sides and drill holes for the 40 mm (1½ in) screws, 10 mm (½ in) in from the tapered edges. Cut four corner supports in sawn timber, each measuring 330 x 25 x 25 mm (13 x 1 x 1 in), and position flush with the pre-drilled sides and top, leaving a 25 mm (1 in) projection at the bottom. Screw in place.

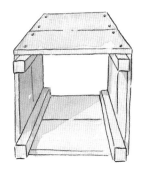

3 Position the longer sides against the outside face of the shorter ones, for a square-ended butt joint. Screw in place, making the holes 40 mm (1½ in) in from the sides of the longer pieces.

4 For the base, take the piece of plywood and cut a 25 x 25 mm (1 x 1 in) square from each corner. Drill five 25 mm (1 in) diameter drainage holes, positioning as shown. Insert the base in position from the bottom of the tub before attaching the four base supports.

5 Cut four base supports 340 x 25 x 25 mm (13½ x 1 x 1 in) in sawn timber and position flush with the bottom edge of the container on all four sides. Secure with 40 mm (1½ in) screws in pre-drilled holes.

6 For the obelisk, cut the following pieces in sawn timber:
• 4 side supports 2350 x 25 x 25 mm (90 x 1 x 1 in)
• 18 m (60 ft) of 25 x 20 mm (1 x 1¾ in) cut into lengths for rungs
• 1 block 100 x 100 x 100 mm (4 x 4 x 4 in) to form tapered top
• 1 board 100 x 100 x 25 mm (4 x 4 x 1 in) to form base of top

7 Place two side supports 100 mm (4 in) apart at the top and 480 mm (19 in) apart at the bottom. Cut and position one rung 130 mm (5 in) from the top and one 150 mm (6 in) from the bottom as shown – make the rungs slightly longer than the actual width. Fix in place with panel pins. Mark the positions of 14 rungs between them at 140 mm (5½ in) intervals. Repeat for the opposite side.

8 Cut and pin 14 rungs to the marked positions then cut off all overhangs flush with the side supports.

9 To assemble the obelisk, lay the two completed sections on their sides and cut and pin a top and bottom rung in place across them, positioning as in step 7. Mark the positions of the rest of the rungs as before then cut and pin them, making sure they line up on all sides. Repeat for the fourth side and cut off the overhangs.

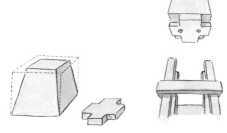

10 For the top, taper the block at an 85° angle. Then cut four 25 x 25 mm (1 x 1 in) squares from the corners of the board. Drill holes in this board and screw to the wide base of the top piece using the 50 mm (2 in) long screws. Slot on top of the main structure and pin to the side supports.

11 Before assembling the whole structure, treat the obelisk and tub with wood preservative. When the surface is dry, apply two coats of coloured wood stain.

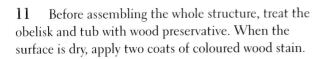

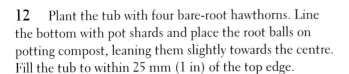

12 Plant the tub with four bare-root hawthorns. Line the bottom with pot shards and place the root balls on potting compost, leaning them slightly towards the centre. Fill the tub to within 25 mm (1 in) of the top edge.

13 To join the tub and obelisk, first cut four battens 400 x 25 x 25 mm (16 x 1 x 1 in). Drill them for 40 mm (1½ in) screws and fix two to opposite sides of the tub; place one flush with the top and the other 130 mm (5 in) below it.

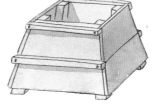

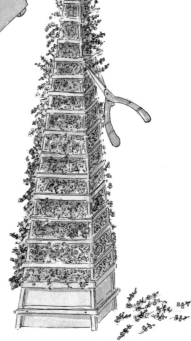

14 Fit the obelisk over the tub, making sure that the structure is square, and screw as above, fixing the bottom two rungs to the battens on the sides of the tub.

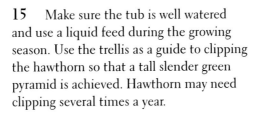

15 Make sure the tub is well watered and use a liquid feed during the growing season. Use the trellis as a guide to clipping the hawthorn so that a tall slender green pyramid is achieved. Hawthorn may need clipping several times a year.

miniature hurdles

Decorative edging adds a finishing touch to borders and paths, defining the boundary between one area and another. An edging can also serve other, practical functions; here, the charming miniature hurdles hold back the plants from the lawn and deter pets from running into the border. Canes can do the same job but they are far less attractive. These decorative hurdles are simple to make – an excellent project for the novice carpenter.

MATERIALS & EQUIPMENT

for each hurdle

2 sweet chestnut uprights 230 mm (9 in) long and 50 mm (2 in) across

5 sweet chestnut crossbars 400 mm (16 in) long and 25 mm (1 in) across

3 sweet chestnut braces 200 mm (8 in) long and 25 mm (1 in) across

galvanized nails

wood preservative

chisel

sharp knife

1   These hurdles are made from sweet chestnut but hazel can also be used. Strip off the bark and split the stems in half lengthways with a knife and chisel.

2   Cut the uprights and crossbars to length. Make a pointed end at the bottom of the uprights and drill five holes through each, starting 50 mm (2 in) from the top and spacing them 50 mm (2 in) apart. Shave the ends of the crossbars to fit into the holes.

3   Put the hurdle together and drill small pilot holes horizontally through the uprights and ends of the crossbars. Secure the structure by carefully hammering small galvanized nails through the pilot holes.

4   Cut the central upright bar and the two diagonals to length, position them, drill pilot holes and secure with galvanized nails. The hurdle now has the appearance of a miniature five-bar gate.

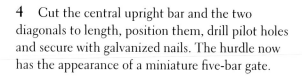

5   The secret to using hurdles is to position them before the plants begin to grow. They will restrain excessive growth but some stems and leaves will grow over and through the hurdles, giving them a natural look. Simply push the hurdles into the soil. In packed soil, pilot holes will help.

alternative edging
Use thin, pliable hazel rods about 1 m (3 ft) long to make hazel hoops. Push one end into the soil and then carefully bend the rod over. Overlap the rods for an elegant, effective finish.

6 Apply a wood preservative that will not harm plants. Periodically check the hurdles for damage and repair or replace any affected parts. Remove the hurdles in the winter, repair any damage, apply a preservative and store them in a dry place.

a picket fence

A picket fence is the ornamental vestige of a defensive palisade in which all the uprights were sharpened to prevent people or animals climbing over. Now the picket fence is a decorative boundary. Its elegant simplicity makes it suitable for formal settings as well as for the exuberance of a cottage garden. Simple flat or pointed pickets are easy to construct if the fence is well planned; for more decorative finials, a mechanical band-saw is useful.

MATERIALS & EQUIPMENT

for each 2 m (6½ ft) section of fence

2 main posts 1.5 m (5 ft) long and 100 mm (4 in) square
(1 for each 2 m (6½ ft) and 1 extra)

13 pickets 1 m x 75 x 10 mm (39 x 3 x ½ in)

2 rails 2 m x 80 x 40 mm (78 x 3 x 1½ in)

45 mm (1¾ in) galvanized nails

½ bucket hardcore per hole

3 buckets concrete per hole

wood preservative

template for picket tops

chisel • spirit level

paint or exterior woodstain (optional)

1   When buying the wood, add 450 mm (18 in) to the length of the posts to secure them in the ground. (See also step 1 on page 110 for determining post length.) Work out the position of the picket panels and, with a chisel, make a slot either side of the posts, 2 mm ($\frac{1}{8}$ in) wider than the bar-end. Treat with preservative and position the first post.

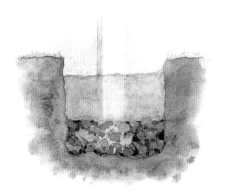

2   Dig a hole 600 mm (24 in) deep and 250 mm (10 in) square, in other words larger than the post. Fill the bottom with hardcore and secure the post with concrete, covering the dry concrete with soil and turf.

3   Make a template for the picket tops and carve them out. Nail the pickets to the horizontal rails to make panels. Space the pickets 80 mm (3 in) apart and position the bars a quarter of the height from the top and bottom. Use galvanized nails, which will not rust.

4   Slot the angled ends of the horizontal bars into the holes on the main post; push them in tightly and nail them in place. The next post should then be positioned. Dig the foundations and add hardcore. Align the post with the first post, align and secure the picket panel and fill the foundation hole.

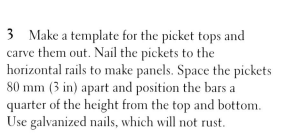

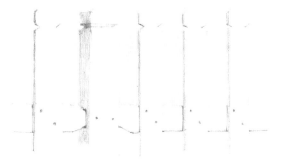

5   Picket fences can be left as natural wood, which can last many years providing the base of the pickets do not touch the ground. Treating the fence with paint or preservative will extend its life; the main posts should always be treated.

simple and decorative finials

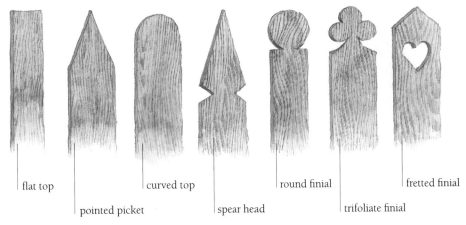

flat top

pointed picket

curved top

spear head

round finial

trifoliate finial

fretted finial

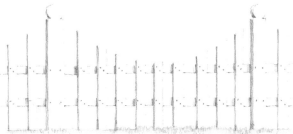

a curved fence

With a little planning, a more elaborate design can be achieved by varying the heights of the pickets and creating a continuous curving finish. The round finials on the posts echo the curve in the picket panels.

a rustic fence

For an informal effect, use natural – but not splintered or coarse – wood and simply nail all the parts together. Less precise measurements are needed so the job is more straightforward, but there is still room for a decorative pattern in the pickets.

wattle panels

To provide an attractive temporary screen, there is nothing better than wattle hurdles. They have a rustic appearance that is effective in less formal settings, and they also work well in modern schemes. Their original purpose was to protect and fence in sheep; today, they can keep pets in or out of a particular part of the garden. Wattle hurdles do not last many years but, providing it is not unstable, an aged panel can be picturesque.

MATERIALS & EQUIPMENT

2 posts 1.8 m (6 ft) for the first panel then 1 per panel

1 wattle panel 1.8 x 1.2 m (6 x 4 ft) for each 1.8 m (6 ft) run

galvanized wire

pliers

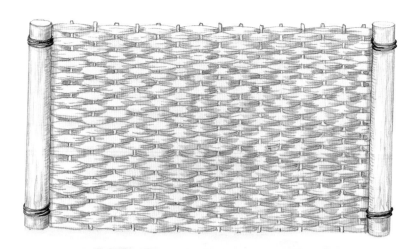

1   For a long-lasting panel, posts should be secured in the ground. For a temporary screen, they can be held firm with rammed earth. Wind wire around the posts and through the panels 100 mm (4 in) from the top and 100 mm (4 in) from the bottom of the panel.

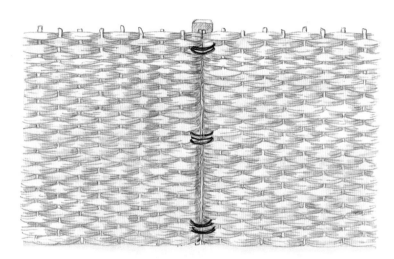

2   Secure the posts as above and bring the edges of the panels together in front of the posts, hiding them. Work the galvanized wire around the post and both panels. Do not leave the end of the wire exposed because this can be dangerous.

3   Untreated wattle panels will last ten years at the most. Treated with a preservative, they will last much longer, but avoid cresote, which can be harmful to plants. In windy situations, use a third length of wire to secure the panels to the posts (as shown in step 2). Check that the posts are secure, particularly where only rammed earth has been used.

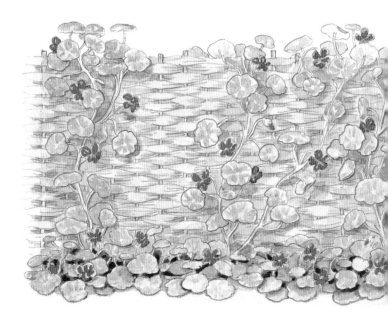

a temporary windbreak

Wattle panels make good windbreaks while a new hedge is growing. Place them about 1 m (3 ft) away from the young plants. The panels should withstand wind, but check them periodically.

a garden screen

Wattle panels can be used as a screen to hide ugly but necessary features such as dustbins and compost heaps. Position the panels so that access is easy and allow plenty of room for manoeuvre for emptying bins or fetching compost. Use a third wire tie to secure the panels because the structure is likely to be knocked in such a situation.

an open wattle fence

For an ideal internal screen, hammer stakes into the ground 300 mm (12 in) apart and weave wands of willow or hazel between them. Weave three or four wands in each direction, twisted to form two 'ropes'.

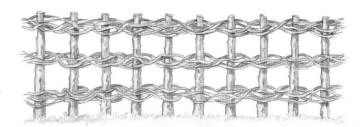

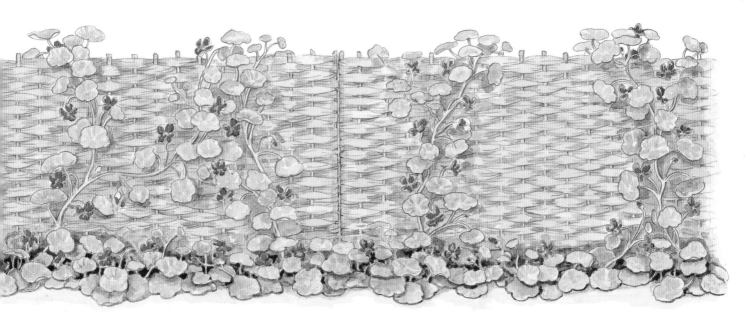

a chequerboard parterre

This project draws on one of the pleasures of gardening: the contrast between formality and luxuriant growth. Ideal for a small garden, the parterre brings order to an otherwise informal setting. The chequerboard effect is based on a design from the 16th and 17th centuries. The herbs are clipped flat and kept square to accentuate the contrasting colours of the herbs and gravel.

MATERIALS & EQUIPMENT

14 m (46 ft) sawn timber 130 x 25 mm (5 x 1 in)

galvanized nails 50 mm (2 in)

1 litre (1¾ pints) clear wood preservative

1 litre (1¾ pints) black wood stain

well-rotted manure

6 heavy-duty black polythene squares 450 x 450 mm (18 x 18 in)

pea gravel

soil-based potting compost

coarse gravel

54 pot-grown rosemary (*Rosmarinus officinalis*)

1   Cut three 1330 mm (52½ in) and two 1780 mm
(70¼ in) boards from the sawn timber. Cut out notches
from the boards as shown. The notches should be
20 mm (¾ in) wide and 60 mm (2½ in) deep. Leave
a gap of 430 mm (17 in) between each notch.

2   Slot the three 1330 mm (52½ in) inner
boards into the notches of the two 1780 mm
(70¼ in) inner boards as shown to create the
inner framework.

3   Cut two 1330 mm (52½ in) outer boards
and two 1823 mm (71¾ in) outer boards
from the sawn timber. Nail these four
boards to the inner framework, as shown,
using 50 mm (2 in) nails. Unless the
sawn timber has already been pressure-
treated, paint the chequerboard parterre
with clear wood preservative.

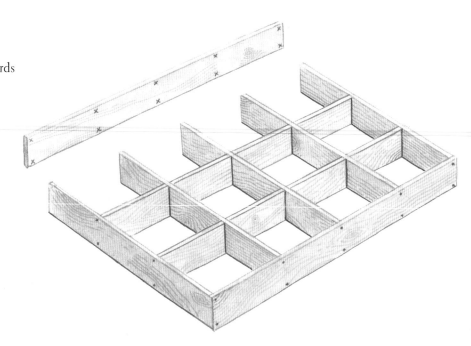

4   Prepare a 1.8 m (6 ft) square plot by digging, weeding
and adding well-rotted manure (see Double Digging, page
250). Paint the parterre with black wood stain before
setting in the ground. Dig out 80 mm (3 in) of soil so that
the parterre is 50 mm (2 in) above soil level.

5 After compacting the earth, line those squares that are to hold the pea gravel with the squares of polythene. Fill each of these squares with pea gravel to 25 mm (1 in) below the top of the parterre. To vary the effect, you can use gravel or coloured or white chippings.

6 Remove the rosemary plants from their pots and plant nine in each of the remaining squares, keeping the finished soil level 25 mm (1 in) below the top of the board. You can also use compact, clippable plants such as rue, santolina or thyme. Clip back the herbs to create the flat, formal effect.

7 The parterre has been surrounded by a band of coarse gravel to act as a textural contrast to the pea gravel in the chequerboard, but it would look equally good set in grass.

herb staging

This semicircular raised herb staging – inspired by the 18th-century staging at the Villa Pisani near Padua, in Italy, where it is used in greenhouses and in an orangery – makes it possible to grow a large collection of plants in a confined space. Two sections of the design can be used back to back to make circular staging. The original staging would have been oak, but the waterproof shuttering ply used here is far cheaper.

MATERIALS & EQUIPMENT

planed timber 4500 x 100 x 50 mm (177 x 4 x 2 in)

exterior-grade plywood 1200 x 600 x 20 mm (48 x 24 x ¾ in)

no. 8 screws 50 mm (2 in) and 100 mm (4 in)

1 litre (1¾ pints) clear wood preservative

1 litre (1¾ pints) dark green matt emulsion

9 clay pots 150 mm (6 in) in diameter and 8 clay pots 200 mm (8 in) in diameter

pot shards

loam-based potting compost

pot-grown culinary herbs (see page 151)

jigsaw with a scrolling blade

long rule

1 To make the front leg, lay a 1 m (39 in) length of planed timber flat on the ground. Using a long rule as a guide, mark out the angles for the cuts by arranging the rule and timber to achieve the configuration shown. The final length of the front leg should be 860 mm (35½ in).

2 The configuration of the back legs is as shown. Cut two 900 mm (36 in) pieces of planed timber and set on the ground as before. Using the long rule as a guide, mark out the angles for the cuts as shown. Note that the back legs butt onto the front leg, so allow for the width of this when marking the angles. The back legs should sit 20 mm (¾ in) down from the top of the long rule.

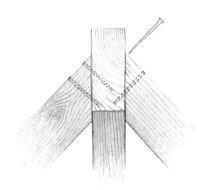

3 Assemble the legs by screwing the two back legs to the front leg using two 100 mm (4 in) screws per leg. Drill the legs as shown. Align the back legs to the front leg 20 mm (¾ in) down from the top of the front leg.

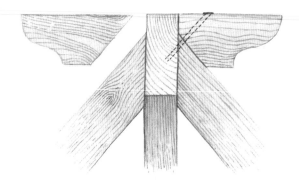

4 Cut nine brackets from the planed timber with the jigsaw and scrolling blade. Position the top shelf brackets first, but cut off a corner from the back leg brackets to a depth of 20 mm (¾ in). Screw the brackets to the legs.

5 Cut out brackets for the middle and lower shelves as before but without cutting off the corners. Position the brackets as shown. On the back legs, from top to bottom, the intervals between the brackets should be 290 mm (11½ in) and 320 mm (12½ in), and the interval between the bottom bracket and the ground should be 260 mm (10¼ in). Drill holes in the brackets and screw to the legs from above. Attach the brackets to the front leg in the same way.

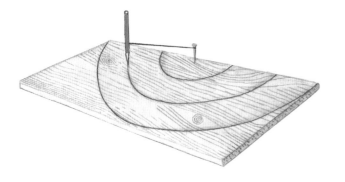

6 To make the shelves, cut three concentric semicircles with radii of 200 mm (8 in), 400 mm (16 in) and 600 mm (24 in) from the plywood. Before cutting, mark the plywood with a felt-tipped pen attached by string to a nail placed in the centre of the long edge of the wood.

7 Screw the top shelf onto the top brackets from above with three 50 mm (2 in) screws. Fix the lower shelves with two screws per bracket. Cover with clear wood preservative, unless the wood is pressure-treated. Paint with the emulsion.

8 The staging can support nine 150 mm (6 in) pots and eight 200 mm (8 in) pots. Other herbs can be potted up and arranged on the ground. Line each pot with pot shards for drainage and pot up the herbs using the compost. Leave a gap of 20 mm (³⁄₄ in) from soil level to the top of the pot.

upper shelf
Nasturtium (*Tropaeolum* 'Alaska')

middle shelf (left to right)
Wild marjoram (*Origanum vulgare*)
Sage (*Salvia officinalis* 'Icterina')
Marjoram (*Origanum vulgare* 'Gold Tip')

lower shelf (left to right)
Golden marjoram (*Origanum vulgare* 'Aureum')
Rosemary (*Rosmarinus officinalis*)
Curly-leaved parsley (*Petroselinum crispum* 'Moss Curled')
Chives (*Allium schoenoprasum*)
Pineapple mint (*Mentha suaveolens* 'Variegata')
Common sage (*Salvia officinalis*)

ground level (left to right)
Spearmint (*Mentha spicata*)
Purple sage (*Salvia officinalis* Purpurascens Group)
Eau de cologne mint (*Mentha* x *piperita* 'Citratra')
Heartsease (*Viola tricolor*)
Summer savory (*Satureja hortensis*)
Golden lemon thyme (*Thymus* x *citriodorus* 'Aureus')
Spearmint (*Mentha spicata*)

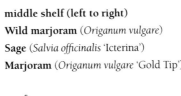

a primula theatre

This design for a primula theatre is for a scaled-down version of an early 19th-century type of shaded staging, made to show off the best examples in a collection and to protect the flowers from sun and rain. It will comfortably hold up to fifteen 100 mm (4 in) pots; terracotta pots look best. Paint or stain the theatre dark blue, dark green, grey or black to form a good background for the rich and varied colours of the primulas.

MATERIALS & EQUIPMENT

planed softwood or sawn timber (see over)

shuttering or other exterior-grade plywood (see over)

sherardized nails and panel pins

waterproof PVA glue

1 litre (1¾ pints) wood preservative or oil-based primer

microporous paint or wood stain

up to 15 terracotta pots with 100 mm (4 in) diameters

Primula vulgaris

P. denticulata

P. veris

P. Gold Lace Group

*Please note: This project is fairly complex. If you do not
have good carpentry skills, you may want to consult a professional.*

1 Cut the wood according to the diagrams and measurements.

front elevation

- 1 top piece 1520 x 560 x 10 mm (60 x 22 x ½ in) plywood A: 1395 mm (55 in), B: 540 mm (21¼ in) C: 200 mm (8 in)
- 2 side pieces 1110 x 150 x 25 mm (43¾ x 6 x 1 in) planed softwood
- 1 bottom piece 1095 x 180 x 25 mm (43 x 7 x 1 in) plywood

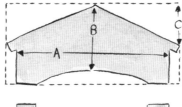

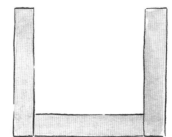

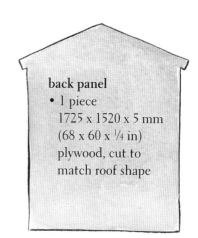

back panel

- 1 piece 1725 x 1520 x 5 mm (68 x 60 x ¼ in) plywood, cut to match roof shape

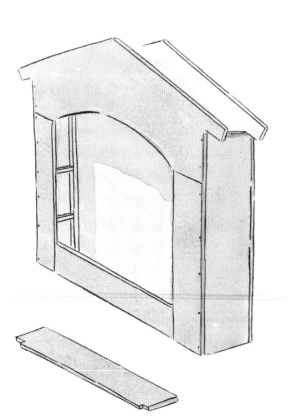

sides and supports

- 2 side panels 1395 x 200 x 10 mm (55 x 8 x ½ in) plywood
- 4 side supports 1395 x 25 x 25 mm (55 x 1 x 1 in) planed softwood
- 6 shelf supports 150 x 25 x 25 mm (6 x 1 x 1 in) planed softwood

2 To make up the sides, glue and nail the side supports to the outer edges of the two side panels. Then pin and glue the shelf supports 150, 480 and 785 mm (6, 19 and 31 in) from the bottom of the side panels. Glue and pin both completed sides to the plywood back.

3 Construct the carcass by attaching the front elevation to the back and sides, pinning and gluing throughout.

4 Cut all the shelves but only attach the bottom one at this stage; sit it on the bottom side supports and pin and glue to the edge of the front elevation.

shelves

- 2 pieces 1370 x 150 x 25 mm (54 x 6 x 1 in) planed softwood
- 1 bottom piece 1395 x 180 x 25 mm (55 x 7 x 1 in) planed softwood with two 25 x 25 mm (1 x 1 in) notches cut from both corners on one long side

5 Secure the roof supports as shown. Wipe off any excess glue. (The actual roof goes on last.)

roof supports

- 6 roof supports 200 x 50 x 50 mm (8 x 2 x 2 in) planed softwood

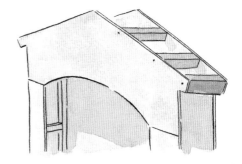

6 Cut out the upper and lower sections of the top pediment from softwood. Secure mitred edges with glue, reinforcing with panel pins. Glue and nail to the carcass in the positions indicated – place the upper section first. (For mitring see page 247.)

top pediment
- 2 upper sections 50 x 50 mm (2 x 2 in), approximately 760 mm (30 in) long to fit the size of the pediment, mitred at one end
- 2 lower sections 25 x 25 mm (1 x 1 in), approximately 760 mm (30 in) long to fit the size of the pediment, mitred at both ends

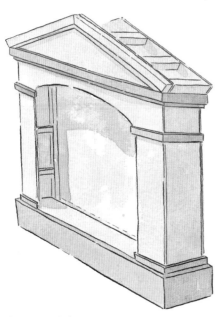

skirting
- 1 piece 1445 x 180 x 25 mm (57 x 7 x 1 in), mitred at both ends
- 2 pieces 260 x 180 x 25 mm (10¼ x 7 x 1 in), mitred at one end

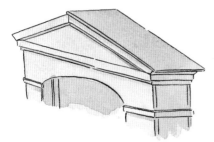

8 Cut out the roof pieces and nail in place, lining up the back edge with the back panel.

- 2 pieces 780 x 305 x 10 mm (30¾ x 12 x ½ in) plywood, mitred at one end

7 Using softwood cut out the base pediment, the capitals, the base column and the skirting, as highlighted in the illustration, from top to bottom. Secure in the same way as for the top pediment (see step 6).

base pediment
- 1 upper section 1495 x 50 x 50 mm (59 x 2 x 2 in), mitred at both ends
- 2 upper side sections 280 x 50 x 50 mm (11¼ x 2 x 2 in), mitred at one end
- 1 lower section 1445 x 25 x 25 mm (57 x 1 x 1 in), mitred at both ends
- 2 lower side sections 260 x 25 x 25 mm (10¼ x 1 x 1 in), mitred at one end

capitals
All pieces to be mitred at one end.
- 2 pieces 245 x 25 x 25 mm (9¾ x 1 x 1 in)
- 2 pieces 200 x 25 x 25 mm (8 x 1 x 1 in)

base column
All pieces to be mitred at one end.
- 2 pieces 245 x 10 x 25 mm (9¾ x ½ x 1 in)
- 2 pieces 180 x 10 x 25 mm (7 x ½ x 1 in)

9 Treat the theatre and shelves with a suitable wood preservative. Finish by painting with a microporous paint or an exterior decorative wood stain. Make sure that the staging is thoroughly dry and aired before placing plants, since preservatives and stains are often toxic to plants. Insert the two remaining shelves. Choose your plants from the selection listed. Plant them in shallow terracotta pots lined with pot shards and display on the staged shelving.

a wirework basket

This unusual wirework basket is inspired by edgings used in the early 19th century to surround and support plants. A galvanized-iron strip at the bottom creates a border around a basket-like stand, which acts as an attractive frame for rambling rose bushes. The best roses to use for this project are low-growing ground-cover ones, but you can adapt the basket to fit larger plants such as shrub roses.

MATERIALS & EQUIPMENT

1 sheet galvanized steel 1200 x 300 mm (48 x 12 in); use a gauge that can be cut with tinsnips

6 galvanized roofing bolts 10 mm (½ in) long and 6 mm (¼ in) wide

22 m (72 ft) galvanized fencing wire 5 mm (⅕ in) thick

1 piece plywood 525 x 350 x 25 mm (21 x 14 x 1 in)

tinsnips

hacksaw and vice or G-cramps

small pot grey-blue metal primer

roll of thin galvanized wire

well-rotted manure and rose fertilizer

5 bare-root roses (*Rosa* 'The Fairy')

1   Cut the sheet of galvanized iron into three strips, each 100 mm (4 in) wide. Cut two strips to a length of 1200 mm (48 in) and one to a length of 600 mm (24 in).

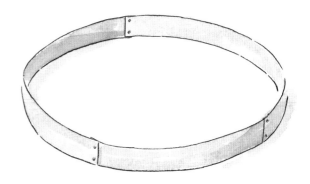

2   Drill two holes 7 mm (⅜ in) in diameter at the ends of each strip. Then connect the three sections together to form a ring by lining up the holes at the ends and securing the joins with roofing bolts through the prepared holes. This strip acts as a template for preparing the bed and as a retainer for the basket.

3   For the basket, cut the fencing wire into 16 pieces, each 1360 mm (54 in) long; use a hacksaw and vice or G-cramp to hold the wire in place.

4   To shape the wire, make a former from the plywood – this will act as a solid pattern around which to bend your wire. Mark the centre point at the top and draw the curved sides to within 200 mm (8 in) of the bottom; this section of the arch remains straight. Cut out the shape with a jigsaw.

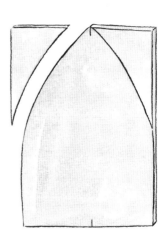

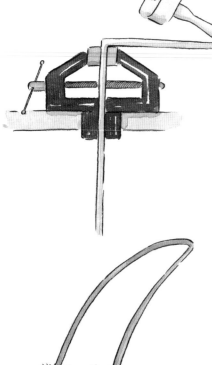

5   Mark the centre point on each length of fencing wire. Using a vice, bend the wire at this point into a right angle; it helps to use a lump hammer as well.

6   Place the right angle of wire over the tip of the former and bend the wire to fit the shape exactly; the wire should extend for about 100 mm (4 in) beyond the bottom edge of the former.

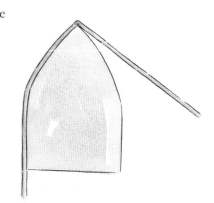

7   Each section of the frame now needs to be bent outwards; turn the arches sideways and use the former to check the curves are all the same.

8   Before constructing the basket shape, paint all the metal components with the metal primer; the grey-blue used here appears as a patinated copper colour and makes a good foil for this planting scheme.

9 Choose an area of flat ground for your rose bed. If the area is grassed over, position the ring and cut around its inner edge to mark the turf; put the ring to one side and remove the turf by dividing it into squares and lifting out with a spade. Turn over the bed and fork in well-rotted manure, then gently press the ring in position.

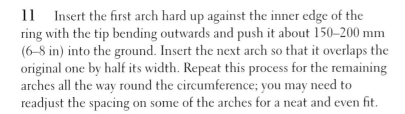

10 Plant the five roses, positioning them as shown left. Make sure that the junctions of stem and root are at surface level. Top dress with rose fertilizer.

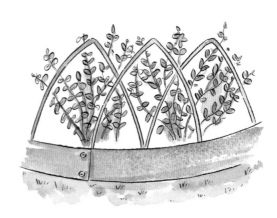

11 Insert the first arch hard up against the inner edge of the ring with the tip bending outwards and push it about 150–200 mm (6–8 in) into the ground. Insert the next arch so that it overlaps the original one by half its width. Repeat this process for the remaining arches all the way round the circumference; you may need to readjust the spacing on some of the arches for a neat and even fit.

12 Secure the basket sections together by twisting the thin galvanized wire around the crossover junctions on each arch.

13 Prune the roses so that they form a slightly domed shape and trim any grass around the outer edge for a formal effect.

alternative planting schemes
For a basket of this size, try the roses 'White Pet' or 'Nozomi', or for a larger arrangement use the pink rose 'Marguerite Hilling' or its creamy white sister 'Nevada'. A suitable shrub would be *Camellia japonica* 'Alba Plena'.

a rose arch

Arches can be put to very effective use in the garden, dividing one area from another, but their greatest asset is that they are ideal as supports for growing climbers. Wooden archways are not difficult to make from scratch. Alternatively, a variety of elegant metal and wooden frames is readily available in easy-to-assemble kit form, so any garden can be given a passageway and a home for delightful climbers.

MATERIALS & EQUIPMENT

wood or metal garden arch (see step 5, page 163)

½ bucket hardcore for each hole

3 buckets concrete for each hole

2 *Rosa* 'Adélaïde d'Orléans'

1 bucket organic material for each plant

plant ties

spirit level

1 An arch on a sheltered site can be stabilized by ramming down the earth around the legs, but an arch on an exposed site must be well secured so that winds combined with the weight of plants do not topple it. Check the manufacturer's recommended depth for sinking the arch.

2 For a larger arch, dig a hole 600 mm (24 in) deep and 200 mm (8 in) square for each leg, fill the bottom of the holes with 150 mm (6 in) of hardcore and sink the arch 450 mm (18 in) into the ground. Check that the arch is straight and secure with concrete, leaving the last 50 mm (2 in) to be covered with soil.

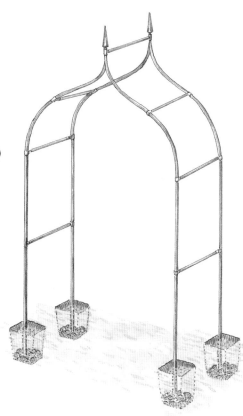

3 Before planting, treat the metal framework with a preservative that will not harm the roses. Plant a climbing or rambling rose on either side – here the rambler *Rosa* 'Adélaïde d'Orléans' – on the outside of the arch, away from any concrete or rammed-earth foundations. Lead the stems, with a cane if necessary, onto the arch and tie the branches in.

4 Prune as for climbing roses on a wall (see page 257), but train them up over the arch rather than fanning them out. Tie in any wandering shoots but do not allow the climbers to become too thick. Take care to remove all dead wood.

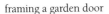

framing a garden door

marking a rise of steps

arching across a path

alternative uses
Rose arches are used as romantic and fragrant
'doorways' from one part of a garden to another,
usually covering a path. They can mark a gateway
through a wall or a hedge or crown the top
of steps, while a series of arches creates
a pergola effect.

5 When you buy or make the
arch, remember that it needs to
be wide enough to walk through
when it is covered with roses.
The flowers can extend 300 mm
(12 in) into the arch from the
sides and the top.

decorative planting projects

a scented knot garden

Knot gardens were among the earliest forms of garden decoration and their attractions are still appreciated today. The hedged patterns may have a medieval feel about them, but they also have a clear-cut quality that appeals to modern gardeners, especially if the hedging is scented. Once created, knot gardens are long-lived features and, although their structure is fixed, their contents and colours can change with the seasons.

MATERIALS & EQUIPMENT

5 plant stakes 900 mm (3 ft) long

5 tree ties

sharp sand (on heavy soils)

pegs and string

plants in variety (see page 168)

well-rotted organic material

1 Careful planning is needed to get the scale and proportions right. For this reason, it is advisable to work out the design on squared paper before planting even a small garden, such as this 4 x 4 m (14½ x 14½ ft) plot. The design can come from your own head or be copied from an historic garden. The pattern can be geometric or include curved flowing lines, as in paisley designs. Simple designs are often most effective; more complicated patterns are best appreciated from upstairs in the house.

2 Prepare the ground thoroughly by removing or killing every piece of perennial weed, and dig in plenty of well-rotted organic matter. Santolina, which makes up the hedges, likes a free-draining soil, so dig in sharp sand to improve drainage if necessary.

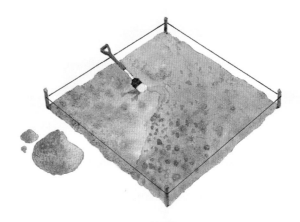

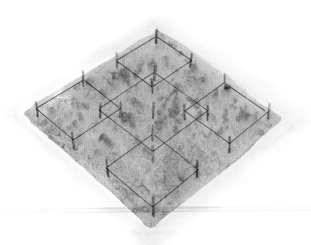

3 Mark out the position of the santolina hedges using pegs and string. If your design involves curves, first draw a grid over your plan, then lay out a similar grid on the ground with pegs and string. Using the grid as a guide, draw the curves on the ground using a bottle filled with dry sand as a marker.

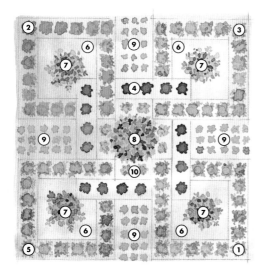

planting scheme

1 *Santolina chamaecyparissus* 'Lambrook Silver' x 19
2 *S. pinnata neapolitana* x 19
3 *S. pinnata neapolitana* 'Sulphurea' x 19
4 *S. rosmarinifolia* x 16
5 *S. chamaecyparissus nana* x 19
6 *Viola* 'Jeannie Bellew' x 100
7 *Rosa* 'Fragrant Cloud' (half-standard) x 4
8 *Ilex aquifolium* 'Silver Queen' (standard) x 1
9 *Chamaemelum nobile* 'Treneague' x 60
10 *Nicotiana* 'Domino White' x 8

4 The planting within the hedged areas is a mixture of tall perennials surrounded by an ever-changing scene of annuals. Here, roses are underplanted with violas in the four outer squares, nicotiana surrounds a holly standard in the centre square, and chamomile lawns fill the open squares.

5 Plant the central holly tree (*Ilex aquifolium*) in spring before setting out the hedges, to avoid damaging the santolina. Dig a large hole and work compost into the base. Spread out the roots, refill and water. Secure the tree to a stake using a tree tie about 300 mm (12 in) above ground.

6 Plant the roses, using either bushes or half-standards; the latter need staking in the same way as the holly standard. Then plant the santolina at 300 mm (12 in) intervals using the strings as a guide. Water well. In an exposed garden, put up a temporary windbreak of plastic netting until the plants are established. Once established the santolina is quite tough and will even withstand sea breezes.

7 Cut back the santolina in spring. If you dislike its combination of yellow flowers and silver foliage, remove the flower buds before they open.

8 The knot garden will seem full of holes when first planted, but the santolina will soon fill out into a thick hedge, which should be kept neatly trimmed. Always remove dead and dying plants from the infill planting: an empty square looks better than one with tatty or dying vegetation.

corner planting

All gardens have odd corners and there are plenty of ways to make imaginative use of them – especially desirable for gardeners who are short of space. Another advantage of filling these corners is that it helps to unify the garden and create an overall picture. A common solution is to use bland ground-cover plants to fill such areas, but it is more rewarding to create something interesting like this simple cool-looking border.

MATERIALS & EQUIPMENT

9 *Alchemilla alpina*

4 *Euphorbia stricta*

3 *Mimulus guttatus*

2 *Deschampsia flexuosa*

1 *Geranium pratense* 'Mrs Kendall Clark'

1 *Alchemilla conjuncta*

gravel

1   Rather than filling awkward corners with containers, make a properly prepared bed for your plants. This will need far less work, particularly when it comes to watering. Finish it with gravel, which acts as a mulch, is a complement to many plants and presents an orderly finish. Gravel can make a highlight of a corner planting, as it does with this 3.5 x 3.5 m (12 x 12 ft) plot.

2   If you are planting close to a wall, avoid using tall plants that may bend forwards, drawn to the light and pushed by winds. Make sure the gravel is well distributed around the plants and that any small rocks are securely bedded in the ground.

3   As an alternative to gravel, you can use paving slabs and plant between them, creating a tapestry of cover. Erigeron, acaena, thyme and mint are useful; the last two are also aromatic.

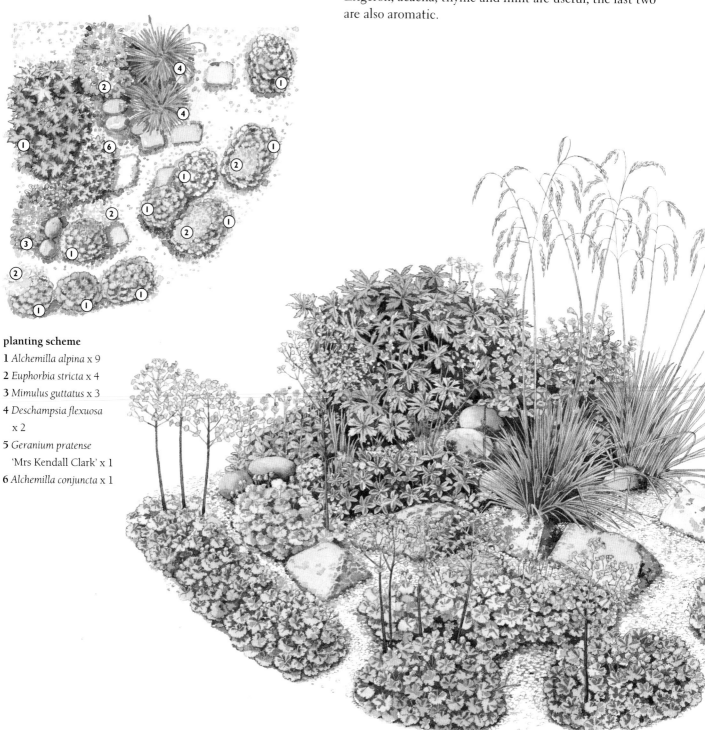

planting scheme
1 *Alchemilla alpina* x 9
2 *Euphorbia stricta* x 4
3 *Mimulus guttatus* x 3
4 *Deschampsia flexuosa*
   x 2
5 *Geranium pratense*
   'Mrs Kendall Clark' x 1
6 *Alchemilla conjuncta* x 1

alternative scheme: a small rock garden

1 A well-constructed, well-planted rock garden is an excellent solution for many corners, but it will need regular weeding, as once weeds have taken hold they can be difficult to remove. Bury at least half of each rock in the soil. This will make it secure and provide a cool, moist rootrun. Arrange rocks in tiers, all leaning back slightly.

2 Rock gardens are intended to replicate rocky outcrops so aim for strata of rocks, leaning at the same slight angle into the ground.

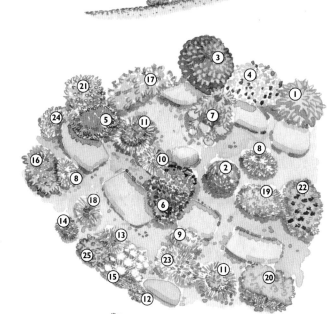

3 When building the garden, never lift more than you can comfortably handle and protect your fingers from crushing stones. Get help if necessary. Move large rocks using a strong pole as a lever, or roll rather than lift them. Make sure all rocks are secure.

alternative planting scheme

1 *Daphne tangutica* x 1
2 *Juniperus communis* 'Compressa' x 1
3 *Picea mariana* 'Nana' x 1
4 *Helianthemum* 'Annabel' x 1
5 *Phlox douglasii* 'Crackerjack' x 1
6 *Aubrieta* 'Joy' x 1
7 *Euphorbia myrsinites* x 1
8 *Lewisia tweedyi* x 2
9 *Erinus alpinus* x 1
10 *Dianthus* 'Little Jock' x 1
11 *Rhodohypoxis baurii* x 2
12 *Armeria juniperifolia* x 1
13 *Pulsatilla vulgaris* x 1
14 *Androsace carnea* subsp. *laggeri* x 1
15 *Achillea clavennae* x 1
16 *Gentiana septemfida* x 1
17 *Convolvulus althaeoides* x 1
18 *Sisyrinchium idahoense* subsp. *bellum* x 1
19 *Hypericum olympicum* 'Citrinum' x 1
20 *Campanula carpatica* x 1
21 *Aster alpinus* x 1
22 *Geranium cinereum* subsp. *subcaulescens* x 1
23 *Dianthus* 'Annabel' x 1
24 *Polygala chamaebuxus* var. *grandiflora* x 1
25 *Erodium corsicum* x 3

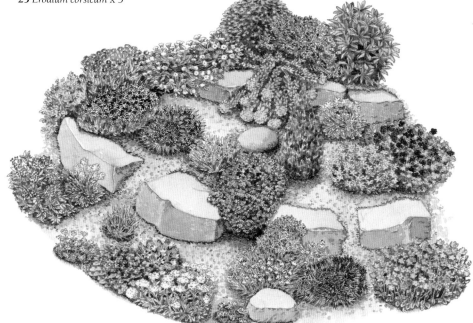

4 The top dressing of gravel will gradually mix into the soil and should be replaced as necessary. Protect any plants that may suffer from winter cold with a sheet of glass or a frame covered with polythene, but allow air to circulate at the sides. Water alpines during dry spells. Trim back straggling plants.

a sweet pea obelisk

The distinctive scent of sweet peas seems to be loved by everyone, probably because it is particularly evocative of childhood. Sweet peas are not just for decorating and perfuming the garden; they also make excellent cut flowers. They are easy to grow from seed and can be used in many decorative ways in the garden, whether you grow them up tripods or allow them to scramble through shrubs with gay abandon.

MATERIALS & EQUIPMENT

seed trays

4 canes or poles 2.5 m (8 ft) long

garden string

sweet pea seed (*Lathyrus odoratus*)

well-rotted organic material

1 In early spring, sow sweet pea seeds into a good compost in cellular trays. If you use fibrous trays the resulting seedlings can be planted out without disturbing the roots. Sow one seed per cell, water and leave in a warm place, out of direct sunlight. Sweet peas can also be bought as seedlings, but growing from seed will give you a much greater choice of colours and scents.

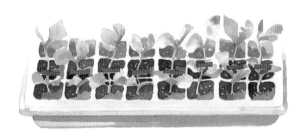

2 When the seedlings have reached 100 mm (4 in), pinch out the tops of the stems just above the nearest set of leaves. If you buy the plants as seedlings, avoid lanky and overcrowded specimens, and watch out for evidence of pests and disease.

3 Prepare the ground thoroughly, removing any weeds and adding plenty of organic material to rejuvenate the soil. Push four canes into the ground (or more for a bigger structure), about 400 mm (16 in) apart, so that their tops meet to form a pyramid. Make certain that each cane is firmly anchored. Tie their tops together in the style of a wigwam.

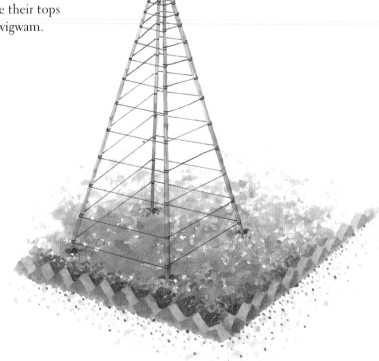

4 Tie string spirally around the obelisk, securing it to each cane as it passes. This is to give the sweet pea plants more to cling to. The string should be strong, but can be made of natural degradable fibres as it does not have to last longer than one season.

5 Plant the sweet peas at 200 mm (8 in) intervals around the base of the obelisk. They will need to be tied to the canes or string to start with, but will soon be self-supporting. Handle the young stems carefully because they may be brittle at this stage. It is wise to put down slug pellets after planting; slugs will eat right through the succulent young pea stems.

6 Sweet peas flower from the summer to early autumn. 'Old-fashioned' varieties produce small but highly scented flowers in blues, reds, pinks and whites. Newer cultivars come in almost all colours and, because they produce larger flowers, they may be more suitable for cutting. Do not let flowers on the plant run to seed – cut them off as they fade.

alternative supports

sweet pea wall
Sweet peas do not have to be trained up an obelisk; a 'wall' of sweet peas can be made by arranging the canes as above. Alternatively, sweet peas can be grown up trellising, wire rings, or through shrubs that have flowered in the spring.

container planting
Sweet peas can be grown successfully in containers. They do best in large pots and should be supported with sticks or a wigwam of poles. Water the container at least once a day, and twice or more on hot, dry days; apply liquid feed every two weeks. Again, the plants should be deadheaded to encourage flowering.

a honeysuckle porch

Honeysuckle is a scent evocative of country lanes, cottage gardens
and romantic trysts. It is particularly pleasing during the evening,
especially as dusk falls. Possibly the best place to grow honeysuckle
is over a summerhouse or a porch, so that the scent wafts
in through the open door on the evening breeze.

MATERIALS & EQUIPMENT

galvanized wire

vine eyes

wall plugs

wooden blocks (see step 4, page 180)

well-rotted organic material

2 honeysuckles (*Lonicera similis delavayi*)

chipped bark mulch

plant ties

bamboo canes

wire cutters

1   Many houses have a side or front porch or an attached building, such as a car port or shed. These are often later additions to the house that add little to its original character. Covering the building with honeysuckle, roses, jasmine or wisteria will help to disguise its appearance and fill the house with scent. Even attractive porches can be enhanced by having honeysuckle growing round them.

2   Climbing plants such as honeysuckle are best supported by horizontal galvanized wires, firmly anchored to the wall at 450 mm (18 in) intervals. Each wire is secured at its ends by vine eyes screwed or hammered into the wall. Bend the wire back on itself, twisting it round with pliers to keep it as taut as possible. The wires and vine eyes can be painted the same colour as the wall to make them less visible.

3   Honeysuckle will clamber over a roof on its own, but wire supports will provide it with better grip in strong winds, especially while it is becoming established. Screw the vine eyes into the barge boards on either side of the porch at 450 mm (18 in) intervals and draw the wire taut over the roof.

4   Use treated wooden spacing blocks to lift the wires off the roof tiles. This gives the honeysuckle more space in which to twine around the wire and protects the tiles from damage. The blocks are made by simply nailing together three pieces of wood in a 'sandwich'. The middle piece should be just a little thicker than a tile, and should be slightly recessed, so that the whole assembly can be slipped over the edges of the tiles.

5   Honeysuckle does not like to be dry at the roots, so add a generous amount of fibrous organic material to the soil at the base of the porch. This fibrous material holds plenty of moisture but allows excess rain to drain away. While digging, make sure that all perennial weeds are removed.

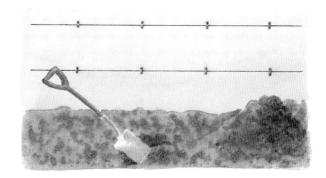

6 Plant one honeysuckle bush on either side of the porch. Dig the planting holes at least 300 mm (12 in) away from the walls. Plant so that the top of the root ball is level with the surface of the soil. Water well and mulch with chipped bark.

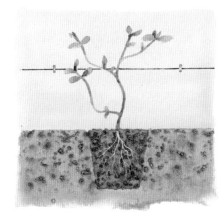

7 Lead the stems towards the wire supports using canes tipped at an angle from the root ball to the wall. Avoid damaging the roots as you push the canes into the ground. Tie the stems to the cane and, when they are larger, directly to the wires.

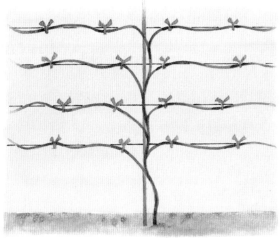

8 Fan out the shoots so that they cover all the wires. Spread out the shoots at the base of the wall; similarly, spread out any side shoots that emerge further up the plant, to cover the entire wall. Tie in the shoots with string or plant ties.

9 Honeysuckle need not be pruned at all, but removing dead material helps prevent a build-up of weight as well as making the plant look fresher and neater.

a rose growing through a tree

Scented climbers rambling up through old trees can be a breathtaking sight. Some of the best climbers for this are the old rambling roses and honeysuckles. Many clematis species are also suitable, although the fragrant varieties tend to be those with small flowers, with the exception of the spring-flowering *Clematis montana*. Always choose a strong, sound tree; never use dead trees because these may break without warning.

MATERIALS & EQUIPMENT

stout rope

rubber padding

plant ties

1 *Rosa* 'Félicité et Perpétue'

two buckets of garden compost

chipped bark mulch

1   When growing a climbing rose up a tree, it is essential to provide support until its questing stems reach the lower tree branches. There are many ways to do this, but one of the most unusual is to use a thick rope. Fasten the rope to one of the main branches, tying it securely but not tightly. Place a sheet of thick rubber between the rope and the branch to protect the bark from chafing. Wrap the rope around the trunk in a loose spiral, allowing room for the trunk to expand without the rope cutting into it. Loosely tie round the bottom of the trunk.

2   Plant the rose about 600 mm (2 ft) from the base of the tree. Dig compost into the soil and plant the rose at the same depth as it was in its pot. If the rose is bare-rooted, plant it to the same depth as it was in the nursery bed (indicated by the soil line on the stem). It is helpful to incline the rose towards the tree, supporting it with a cane during the first months of growth. Water thoroughly and mulch with composted or chipped bark.

3   Train the stems up to the rope and attach with plant ties. As the stems grow, continue to tie in. Regularly check to ensure the rope is not constricting or chafing the tree. Cut out any dead wood from the rose and, from time to time, remove one or more of the oldest stems to encourage new growth from the base. Tie these new shoots in, either to the rope or to the other stems.

4 Eventually the rose will reach up into the tree and become self-supporting. New shoots from the base will grow up through the increasing mass of stems, and only the more wayward will need tying in. The rope can then be detached, or left in place if it is causing the tree no problem. It will take some years before the tree is completely covered – but the wait is worthwhile.

alternative rose supports

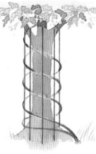

fan support
One way to support a rose before it reaches the lower tree branches is to push long canes into the ground so that they extend from the rose into the lower branches.

pole cage
Another way is to place canes all round the tree about 150 mm (6 in) from the trunk and train the shoots in a spiral around the 'cage'. Support the canes with hoops of wire.

visible trunk
To keep the tree trunk visible, grow the rose up a single pole placed 600 mm (2 ft) from the trunk. Don't attach anything constricting to the tree or drive nails into its trunk.

185

a scented path

Borders that line paths are always welcome as they bring the viewer close to the plants. This is doubly rewarding with fragrant borders as the sense of smell as well as that of sight is stimulated; in many cases, the action of rubbing against the plants as you pass produces the fragrance. Lavender and rosemary have very distinctive, strong aromas that pervade the air for a long distance, far beyond the pathway.

SCENTED PLANTS TO USE

fragrant foliage	fragrant flowers	
Aloysia triphylla	Berberis	Lupinus
Artemisia	Choisya ternata	Matthiola
Lavandula	Convallaria majalis	Nicotiana
Mentha	Daphne	Osmanthus
Monarda didyma	Dianthus	Philadelphus
Myrtus communis	Erysimum	Reseda odorata
Origanum	Hesperis matronalis	Rhododendron (azaleas)
Rosmarinus	Hyacinthus	Rosa
Salvia officinalis	Iris unguicularis	Sarcococca
	Lathyrus odoratus	Syringa
	Lilium	Viburnum
		Viola odorata

1 Fragrant plants add a special dimension to the garden. Many plants, such as lavender, produce the most wonderful perfumes, which are perfect for creating a relaxing atmosphere. Lavender is shown here; more suggestions are given on page 186. This delightful path is 7.5 x 2.5 m (25 x 9 ft).

2 Most garden paths should be wide enough for two people to walk side by side; allow at least 1.5 m (5 ft). Paths that are purely for access can be narrower but should still be able to take a wheelbarrow comfortably. For this scented path there should be adequate room in the beds on either side for the lavenders to grow without overhanging the path too far. As a general rule, borders should be twice as wide as the height of the tallest plants to be used.

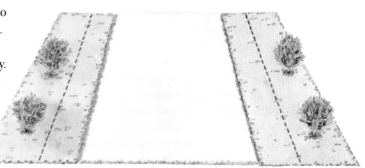

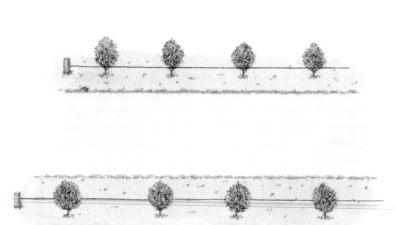

3 Using a string line as a guide, plant the lavenders in a straight row, each being close enough to the next to merge with it when in full growth, that is 600 mm (2 ft) all round. To make a consistent picture, use the same-coloured variety for all the plants. Seed-grown plants may be cheaper, but the colours can vary. Plant the shrubs to the same depth as they were in their pots, firm down and water. If possible, mulch the plants to retain moisture and to keep down weeds.

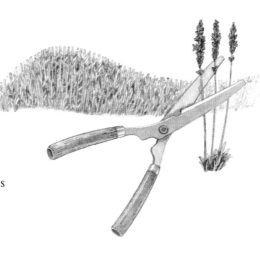

4 Lavender should be sheared over in late summer. Remove all flower stems and cut away about 25 mm (1 in) of the previous season's growth. Shape the border into a slightly undulating, low hedge.

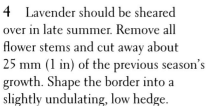

alternative pathway

In cottage-style gardens plants often spill over the edges of paths. Paths for this kind of border should be wide enough to accommodate both the spreading plants and the passage of people. Typical fragrant plants for this type of display are border pinks, especially the old-fashioned varieties.

alternative planting scheme

1 *Lupinus* 'Kayleigh Ann Savage' x 1

2 Chives x 3

3 *Dianthus* 'Haytor White' x 1

4 Thyme x 1

5 Sage x 1

6 *Dianthus* 'Gran's Favourite' x 2

7 *Artemisia caucasica* x 1

8 *Alchemilla mollis* x 2

9 *Geranium sanguineum* 'Album' x 1

10 Mint x 1

11 *Dianthus* 'Laced Monarch' x 1

12 *Tanacetum parthenium* 'Aureum' x 1

herb topiary

Woody-stemmed herbs trained as decorative topiary specimens for containers add formal structure to an established herb bed or act as a focal point flanking an entrance or seat. Rosemary is particularly good for training into a half-standard. A native of the Mediterranean, it grows well and looks attractive in terracotta. You can also train sweet bay and myrtle into topiary half-standards and herbs such as lavender into small topiary balls.

MATERIALS & EQUIPMENT

1 young pot-grown rosemary (*Rosmarinus officinalis*)

1 terracotta pot 280 mm (11 in) in diameter

1 litre (1¾ pints) soil-based potting compost

1 cane 600 mm (24 in)

coated wire or plastic ties

small hand shears or scissors

1 Choose a rosemary plant with a strong, single leader. Plant in the 280 mm (11 in) terracotta pot using the compost. Push the 600 mm (24 in) cane, which marks the final height of the half-standard, into the pot and tie loosely to the single leader using coated wire or plastic ties. Take care not to damage the bark.

2 Cut off all the side shoots using small hand shears or scissors to direct the plant's energy up the main stem. Leave a sufficient number of shoots at the top of the stem in order to sustain the plant and to encourage vigorous growth in the crown.

3 In the second year, when the stem of the rosemary has reached the required height of 400 mm (16 in) above the level of the soil, cut out the top of the lead shoot. This cut marks the approximate base of the final crown.

4 Let several top shoots develop. Once they have reached a length of 80–100 mm (3–4 in), cut out the end of each top shoot. Keep the main stem clear of any side shoots.

5   During spring and summer, when the new growth occurs, continue to pinch out the ends of the top shoots once they have grown by 80–100 mm (3–4 in) to achieve a dense and shapely head. You can collect the rosemary clippings for use in the house.

6   Each year start clipping the rosemary standard in mid-spring and trim throughout the growing season in order to keep a tight head. Underplant with pansies (*Viola* x *wittrockiana*) to add further decoration around the edge of the pot.

7   Water regularly and thoroughly, especially if it is sunny or windy. Clip throughout the growing season and remove any leaves from the stem. Feed fortnightly with liquid fertilizer during the growing season. Unless they are frost-proof, the terracotta pots should be brought indoors in winter.

8   In spring transplant pot-bound plants to a larger pot or top dress with fresh compost, organic matter and slow-release fertilizer.

edible planting projects

baskets of tomatoes

In a small garden, every square inch can be exploited to produce vegetables. Vertical space can be filled using hanging baskets and window boxes; and with careful choice of plants, the baskets can be attractive as well as productive. Here tomatoes have been mixed with flowering and foliage plants, but they can be grown alongside other vegetables if space allows. Several baskets in a group, hung at different heights, make an impressive display.

MATERIALS & EQUIPMENT

for each basket

liner

galvanized eye and hook

compost

slow-release fertilizer or liquid feed

1 tomato 'Tumbler'

2 *Petunia* 'Purple'

2 variegated plectranthus (*Plectranthus coleoides* 'Variegatus')

craft knife

1 Hanging baskets are available in a range of materials and designs. Wire baskets are inexpensive and light, but wrought-iron, terracotta, wicker or wooden baskets may be preferred for aesthetic reasons. Before a basket can be filled and planted, it must be lined.

2 Fit the lining, which may be of fibre, moulded paper, moss or polythene; polythene is ugly if not completely covered by plants. The lining is likely to be porous, so drainage is not a problem. It is easier to work on the basket if it is supported on a bucket, particularly if a heavier basket is used.

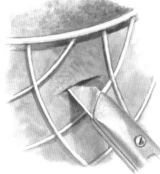

3 Hanging vegetable baskets look their best when completely covered with plants, so it helps to plant the sides as well as the top. Use a craft knife to cut holes or slits in the liner before pouring in the compost. Make the holes no bigger than necessary to push the plant through.

4 Fill the basket with compost to just below the level of the slits in the lining. Wrap the roots of the petunia plants in damp tissue to prevent damage, then push the young plants through the holes in the lining, spreading their roots. Fill the basket with compost. Petunias make a decorative display, but productive plants such as lettuces can be substituted if you prefer.

5 Plant the tomato in the centre of the basket, so that it will hang down on all sides. The variety called 'Tumbler' has been specially developed for planting in hanging baskets.

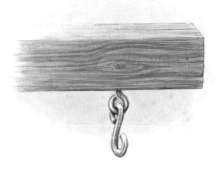

6 Baskets with tomatoes should be hung in a warm, sunny position. If there is an existing beam, then a stout eye screwed into the woodwork will be enough support. Make sure that the beam is strong and in good repair. The basket can be hung at any height. Lower is easier for care and maintenance, but baskets usually look best when above eye-level.

7 Hanging a basket above head height makes watering difficult. One solution is to use a pump-action water dispenser with a long, bent lance. Unless it is raining, baskets should be watered at least once a day; twice on hot days. They also need regular feeding. A slow-release fertilizer can be incorporated in the compost, or liquid feed can be added to the water. Harvest fruit as it ripens and remove any that is damaged or over-ripe.

8 Vegetable baskets look especially attractive in groups of three or more. Hang them at different heights for the best effect. For variety, hang one basket below another.

alternative planting scheme
Instead of tomatoes, plant the basket with cut-and-come-again lettuces. There are varieties available with red foliage and with crinkly and oak-leaf-shaped leaves. A surprising number can be included in the basket if planted round the sides as well as on top. The result will be a ball of colourful lettuce.

chillies in pots

Pot-grown chillies make a spectacular display. There is a wide range of varieties producing yellow, orange, red or purple fruit in bushes of different sizes; in some cultivars the chillies hang from the branches, and in others they are borne upright. Chillies grow slowly in temperate climates; the first fruits appear about 15 weeks after planting. They start green but redden – and grow hotter – as they ripen.

MATERIALS & EQUIPMENT

seed trays

sowing compost

75 mm (3 in) pots for seedlings

large terracotta pots

pot shards

potting compost

chilli plants in variety or seed of several varieties

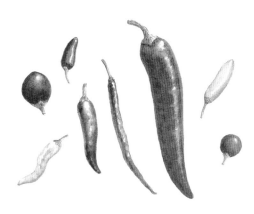

1   Chillies are branching perennials; they vary in size and shape according to variety but can grow to a height of 1.5 m (5 ft). They cannot tolerate low temperatures, so must be started off in a greenhouse or conservatory and not placed outside until the threat of frost has passed.

2   If you cannot buy young plants, chillies may be grown from seed, which is more readily available. Sow seed in trays in early to mid-spring and place in a warm spot or propagator at about 21°C (70°F). Don't let the seed dry out. There should be no need to water seed in a propagator.

3   When the plants are large enough to handle, prick them out into individual pots and grow on in a warm environment. Avoid placing the pots in a cold draught and beware of frost.

4   Terracotta pots are perfect for growing chillies; ideally, use pots that are less than 450 mm (18 in) across because they are light enough to be moved inside during cooler weather. The pots must have a hole in the bottom to allow excess water to drain away.

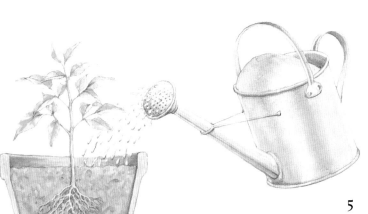

5   Once the plants are about 100 mm (4 in) high, plant them into their final pots. Crock the bottom of the pot with stones or broken pot pieces; fill with a good-quality compost and plant the chilli. Water well. If using large pots, place them in their final position before filling with compost; moist compost adds greatly to the weight.

6 When the plants reach a height of about 150 mm (6 in), pinch off their growing tops to make them bush out. Chillies need a sheltered site and should be placed against a south-facing wall, which will radiate heat during the night, helping to keep the plants warm. Plants should be taken indoors if the temperature drops below 18°C (65°F). Sweet peppers will tolerate slightly cooler conditions and can be used instead.

7 If the plants you have chosen are about the same height, use some form of staging – such as bricks or inverted pots – to vary the level. This will display the plants to best effect and let light through to the plants at the back. The plants will need watering every day and perhaps twice a day in very hot weather. High-potash liquid feed should be added to the water every 10 days once the fruit has started to swell.

8 The fruit can be picked as soon as it is large enough. It can be picked at the green stage when it will be at its mildest, or at its final coloured stage (red, yellow or purple), when it will be hotter. Pick the chillies with part of the stalk still attached. Be certain to have picked all the fruit, or have moved the plants inside, before the first frosts.

a patio container garden

Ordinary terracotta pots, strawberry pots, half-barrels and grow-bags can be used to transform the smallest paved patio into a kitchen garden capable of producing vegetables, fruit and herbs of the highest quality. A well-designed patio kitchen garden can also be an attractive feature in its own right. Virtually any fruit or vegetable can be grown there, although, for obvious reasons, it is advisable to choose the less rampant varieties.

MATERIALS & EQUIPMENT

variety of terracotta pots

potting compost

broken crocks or stones

600 x 50 mm (24 x 2 in) plastic drainpipe

plants in variety

pickaxe

1 A paved patio provides many opportunities for planting crops for the table. Conventional terracotta pots and strawberry pots are attractive, versatile and free-draining; larger containers can be made from half-barrels; and many vegetables thrive in grow-bags. Spreading plants are best planted directly into the ground: use a pickaxe to lift a few of the paving slabs.

2 Remove any rubble and sand from beneath the lifted slabs. Break up the soil below this and fill the remaining space with fresh soil or compost. Plant spreading herbs such as thyme and marjoram and water well.

3 Most vegetables will grow well in pots, even small containers. Crock the bottom of the pot and fill with a good, fresh compost. Sow the seed thinly on the top and cover with a thin layer of compost. Cover the pot with netting to prevent birds or animals from disturbing the compost.

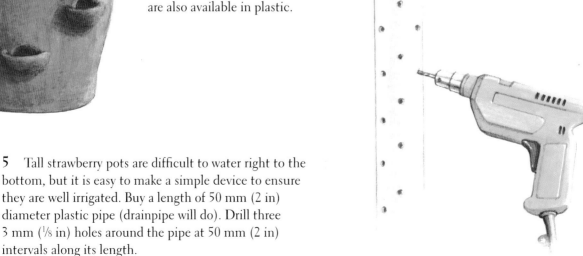

4 There are several types of strawberry pot available; the most decorative are tall terracotta towers that have planting holes in the sides as well as on top. Strawberry towers are also available in plastic.

5 Tall strawberry pots are difficult to water right to the bottom, but it is easy to make a simple device to ensure they are well irrigated. Buy a length of 50 mm (2 in) diameter plastic pipe (drainpipe will do). Drill three 3 mm (⅛ in) holes around the pipe at 50 mm (2 in) intervals along its length.

6   Place the pipe in the centre of the pot and fill around it with compost until you reach the first hole in the side of the pot. Ease the strawberry roots through the hole and continue to fill with compost until the next hole is reached. Plant more strawberries until the pot is full.

7   Fill up the pipe with water, and water the top of the pot. If the bottom of the tube is not in tight contact with the bottom of the pot, the water may run out too quickly. If this is the case, slow down its release by ramming a ball of crumpled polythene down the tube. This will slow the flow sufficiently to allow water to percolate out of the side holes. Water the pot regularly so that it never dries out.

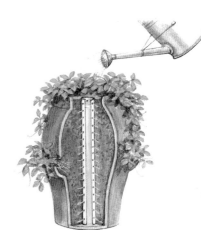

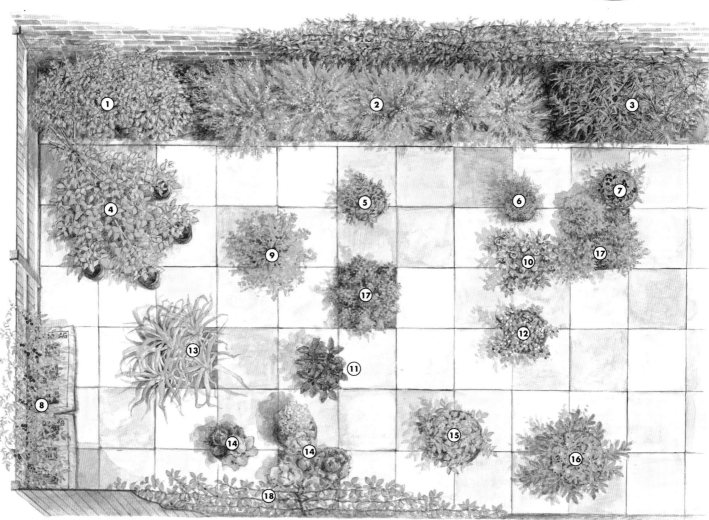

8   Water the pots every day and feed with a liquid feed once a week. Keep the plants neat, removing diseased individuals on sight. Harvest vegetables and fruit as required; avoid leaving over-ripe and rotting produce on the plants.

planting scheme

1 Lemon balm	6 Carrots	10 Patio rose	15 Potatoes
2 Rosemary	7 Bush tomatoes	11 Beetroot	16 Courgettes
3 Lemon verbena	8 Cordon	12 Strawberries	17 Marjoram
4 Runner beans	tomatoes	13 Leeks	18 Pear tree
5 Sage	9 Gooseberries	14 Lettuce	

fruit trees in pots

Fruit is usually associated with large bushes or even huge trees, but most varieties
have dwarf forms that grow well in containers; there are even apple trees that can be
grown as patio plants. However, it is the more exotic fruit, such as oranges and lemons,
that are especially good in containers. This is partly because they are easier to look after
if they can be moved in and out of doors, but also because they are very decorative.

MATERIALS & EQUIPMENT

terracotta pots

stones for drainage

potting compost

young fruit trees and plants (see page 211)

1 Pots should be considered from a practical as well as aesthetic perspective. Plastic pots are much lighter than terracotta but are easier to over-water and provide less thermal insulation for a plant's roots in winter. Terracotta pots look better with the Mediterranean fruit trees used here. They are cooler in summer and warmer in winter, and are heavier than plastic, which means that they are less likely to fall over in a wind; however, they are more difficult to move when full of compost.

2 Crock the bottom of the pots well to aid drainage. Partly fill with compost; place the plant in and fill up to the top with compost. Firm down and water.

3 While most exotic fruit trees need winter protection, they can be placed outside during the summer, preferably against a south-facing wall. This not only provides a good backdrop, but also acts as a storage heater at night. Placing them in a corner offers even better protection. Avoid locations overshadowed by other buildings or trees, or those which funnel draughts over the trees. Containers should be watered every day, and at least twice on hot days or when there is a drying wind. Add liquid feed to the water once a month.

4 The plants used are all perennials and so need to be potted on every year into larger pots until they reach their maximum size. Remove them from their existing pot and shake off any loose compost around the root ball. As the plants grow towards their maximum size, some of the roots can be trimmed back. Repot into a pot one size larger using fresh compost and water well.

5 In temperate climates, oranges, lemons and limes can be grown purely as ornamentals, but they will fruit if given enough warmth. To maximize fruiting in cooler areas, the plants, in their pots, should be kept in a greenhouse or conservatory to provide them with extra warmth. A few pots of smaller plants will act as fillers around the edge of the group; climbers provide a backdrop for the group.

planting scheme
1 Calamondin orange
(*Citrofortunella microcarpa*)
2 Natal plum
(*Carissa grandiflora*)
3 Meyer's lemon
(*Citrus meyeri* 'Meyer')
4 Variegated lemon
(*Citrus limon* 'Variegata')
5 Assorted low-growing ornamentals
6 Rosemary
(*Rosmarinus officinalis*)
7 Wisteria (*Wisteria floribunda*)

6 Most exotic fruit trees and bushes are not winter hardy and so need to be moved under cover – a warm greenhouse or conservatory is ideal. The plants should be kept inside until all possible threat of frost has passed and the daytime temperature reaches an average of 20°C (68°F). Be careful not to over-water during the winter – just keep the soil barely moist.

alternative planting scheme
Less exotic fruits are hardier and can be left outside as long as their containers do not freeze solid. Protect the containers by wrapping straw or bubble wrap around them when cold weather is forecast. Remove the wrapping in warm weather.

1 Pole apple
2 Standard gooseberry
3 Blueberry
4 Strawberry tower
5 Rosemary
6 Assorted low-growing ornamentals

culinary herb half-barrels

These half-barrels are the perfect containers in which to grow a selection of
culinary herbs in even the tiniest of gardens, whether you have a small courtyard
or simply a balcony. The planting schemes create attractive displays and provide
a source of fresh produce for the kitchen. You could also grow other culinary
herbs such as borage, dill and caraway.

MATERIALS & EQUIPMENT

3 half-barrels 300 mm (12 in), 475 mm (19 in), 600 mm (24 in) in diameter

dark grey metal primer

1 litre (1¾ pints) dark green emulsion paint

180 litres soil-based potting compost

plastic pots (see pages 214–215)

pot-grown culinary herbs (see pages 214–215)

1 Choose three identical coopered half-barrels with different diameters. Paint the metal hoops that encircle the half-barrels with dark grey metal primer and then paint the half-barrels and the metal hoops with the dark green emulsion paint. The paintwork should remain weather-proof for a fairly long time, but may need repainting if the paint starts to blister or crack.

2 If there are not already drainage holes in the base of the half-barrels, drill three 25 mm (1 in) holes in each barrel using a flat bit in an electric drill or a brace and bit.

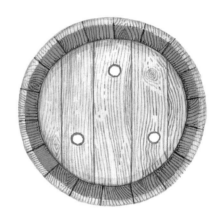

3 Follow the appropriate planting plan for each half-barrel. Remove the herbs from their pots and fill each half-barrel with potting compost so that when you sit the tallest herb on the compost the soil level is approximately 25 mm (1 in) below the top of the half-barrel. Fill in with more compost, and plant the smaller herbs in the same way.

small barrel

Golden thyme
(*Thymus vulgaris aurea*)
x 2, in 130 mm (5 in) pots

Stonecrop
(*Sedum acre*) x 5, in 80 mm (3 in) pots

medium barrel

French parsley
(*Petroselinum crispum*
'Italian') x 1, in an 80 mm
(3 in) pot

Purple sage
(*Salvia officinalis*
Purpurascens Group)
x 1, in a 130 mm
(5 in) pot

White thyme
(*Thymus vulgaris albus*)
x 1, in a 130 mm (5 in) pot

Bronze fennel
(*Foeniculum vulgare* 'Purpureum')
x 3, in 80 mm (3 in) pots

Purple sage
(*Salvia officinalis*
Purpurascens Group)
x 1, in a 130 mm (5 in) pot

Lemon thyme
(*Thymus* x *citriodorus*
'Archer's Gold') x 1,
in a 130 mm (5 in) pot

French parsley
(*Petroselinum crispum*
'Italian') x 1, in an
80 mm (3 in) pot

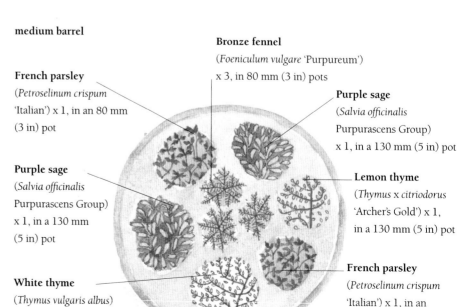

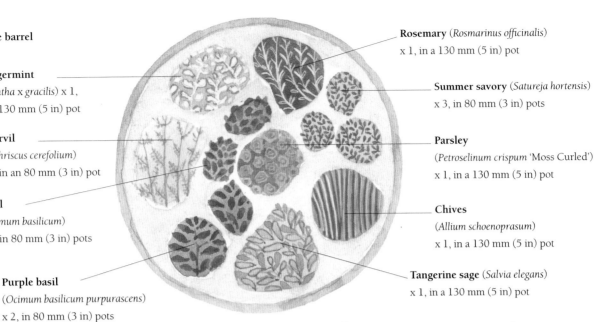

large barrel

Gingermint
(*Mentha* x *gracilis*) x 1,
in a 130 mm (5 in) pot

Chervil
(*Anthriscus cerefolium*)
x 1, in an 80 mm (3 in) pot

Basil
(*Ocimum basilicum*)
x 2, in 80 mm (3 in) pots

Purple basil
(*Ocimum basilicum purpurascens*)
x 2, in 80 mm (3 in) pots

Rosemary (*Rosmarinus officinalis*)
x 1, in a 130 mm (5 in) pot

Summer savory (*Satureja hortensis*)
x 3, in 80 mm (3 in) pots

Parsley
(*Petroselinum crispum* 'Moss Curled')
x 1, in a 130 mm (5 in) pot

Chives
(*Allium schoenoprasum*)
x 1, in a 130 mm (5 in) pot

Tangerine sage (*Salvia elegans*)
x 1, in a 130 mm (5 in) pot

4 Clip back the purple sage each autumn and
replace the biennial parsley once or twice a year to
keep the herbs to a manageable size. Replace the
annual basil every year when the frosts are
definitely over. Sow chervil twice a year if you want
a winter supply. Stonecrop needs to be kept dry.

alternative planting schemes
Other herbs can be planted in the half-barrels,
including marigolds (*Calendula officinalis*) and
heartsease (*Viola tricolor*), as in the small barrel
shown below, and the standard golden bay
(*Laurus nobilis* 'Aurea') in the medium barrel.
Nasturtiums or hops (*Humulus lupulus*) trained
up a bamboo wigwam are an excellent way of
bringing height to a display.

an edible border

Most kitchen produce comes from the vegetable and herb gardens, but there is plenty that can be grown in the more ornamental parts of the garden. Some flowers can be eaten or used as a garnish to food, while many vegetables are so decorative they more than earn their place in the borders. Creating a border with culinary value as well as decorative worth can be very enjoyable and provides great economy of space in a small garden.

PLANTING SCHEME

60 *Atriplex hortensis* 'Rubra' (red mountain spinach)

30 *Calendula officinalis* (pot marigold)

6 *Cynara cardunculus* (cardoon)

20 *Helianthus annuus* (sunflower)

8 *Hemerocallis* (daylily)

1 The unexpected presence of decorative vegetables in a flower border can give freshness to a traditional planting. The soil for such a border can be prepared in the same way as any other border and the planting and maintenance are just the same. These beds measure 6 x 1.8 m (20 x 6 ft). All the edible plants in them will enhance a salad, while the opening buds of the daylily can be chopped up and stir-fried.

planting scheme

1 *Atriplex hortensis* 'Rubra' (red mountain spinach: edible young leaves) x 60

2 *Calendula officinalis* (pot marigold: edible flowers) x 30

3 *Cynara cardunculus* (cardoon: edible blanched stems) x 6

4 *Helianthus annuus* (sunflower: edible seed) x 20

5 *Hemerocallis* (daylily: edible opening buds) x 8

2 Where only parts of plants are being harvested, take from a different plant each time so that there is time for regrowth and you do not create an unbalanced appearance in the bed.

3 Not all garden plants are edible. Only those known to be safe should be eaten or used as food decoration.

alternative edible plants

The list of plants that are edible in whole or part is very long. Here are some of the most rewarding, both in terms of their decorative qualities and for culinary purposes. The less familiar edible parts of some popular vegetables are pointed out.

vegetables

Carrots (foliage)

Swiss chard (foliage)

Tomatoes (fruit)

Peas (flowers and fruit)

Sweetcorn (foliage)

Lettuce (bronze foliage)

flowering plants

Mentha (mint: leaves)

Viola odorata (sweet violets: flowers)

Tropaeolum majus (nasturtium: flowers)

Thymus (thyme: leaves)

Borago officinalis (borage: flowers)

Rosa (roses: petals)

Rosmarinus officinalis (rosemary: flowers, leaves)

pergola planting

1   A pergola, be it a substantial wooden structure or a more refined metal frame, should complement the pathway borders; here, use edible plants.

2   A pergola straddling a path (as left) allows the addition of several types of vegetables or fruit. The overall effect is that of an avenue of produce through which a shady walk can be taken. For a temporary display, runner beans, climbing French beans or marrows and courgettes can be grown. For a more permanent display, grapes (right), apples or pears can be trained over the arches, or a combination of apples and pears (above). Keep the climbers well trained and pruned to get the best from them. This should also allow more light to reach the plants in the borders than if the climbers are neglected.

a salad bed

All vegetables are best eaten fresh, and salad plants in particular are crispest and most flavoursome immediately after picking. Growing your own is very satisfying and lets you harvest as much or as little as you want. It also allows you to combine, in a single salad, the flavours of a wide variety of lettuces – a much more economical option than buying a commercially prepared mixed salad.

MATERIALS & EQUIPMENT

garden line or pegs and string

seed of salad vegetables in variety

well-rotted organic material

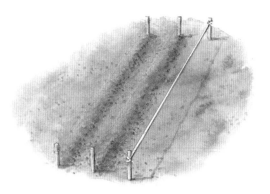

1   Prepare the soil by digging thoroughly and working in plenty of organic material. Using a garden line, mark out the rows, allowing for the size of the full-grown plant plus 300 mm (12 in) between each row for easy access. If you do not have a ready-made garden line, pegs and string can be used in the same way.

2   Using the edge of a hoe, make a shallow channel, or drill, along the lines marked out. Scatter seed evenly along the drill, cover with soil and firm down gently before watering. In very wet conditions, line the drill with dry sand before sowing; in dry conditions water the drill before sowing and lightly press the seeds down into the soil.

3   Even when sown sparingly, most salad crops will need thinning out. When the seedlings are big enough to handle, pull out surplus plants, leaving single plants at the required intervals (equivalent to the width of a mature plant). Most salad crops do best if they are kept growing – any check in growth will affect size and taste – so keep the plants well watered in dry weather. The best method is to water each row individually with a watering can, making certain that the soil is thoroughly soaked.

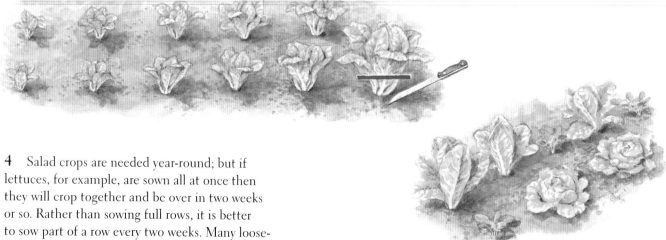

4   Salad crops are needed year-round; but if lettuces, for example, are sown all at once then they will crop together and be over in two weeks or so. Rather than sowing full rows, it is better to sow part of a row every two weeks. Many loose-leaf 'salad bowl' lettuce varieties resprout to give a second or even third crop when cut at the base. Such cut-and-come-again varieties are an excellent way of making use of limited space.

5   Harvesting salad crops inevitably leaves ugly gaps in the rows. To make the best use of space these can be filled by sowing radish seed; radishes are quick to mature and are ready for the kitchen just 3–4 weeks after sowing.

6 Perhaps the most destructive salad crop pests are slugs. An effective way to kill them is to set a beer trap – a jar, partly filled with beer, set into the soil. Alternatively, simply remove the slugs from the plants at night, when they are most active.

planting celery
Dig plenty of manure into the soil – celery demands high levels of nitrogen. Raise young celery plants from seed in the greenhouse. In spring, set these small plants out in a narrow trench.

7 Hoe along the rows and round each plant to remove weeds. Leaf vegetables cannot be stored; cooked puréed tomatoes can be frozen; celery can be left in the ground until needed.

blanching celery
When the celery reaches a height of about 300 mm (12 in), wrap corrugated cardboard round the stems, leaving the leaves free. Fill the trench with earth, drawing it up around the cardboard 'sleeve'.

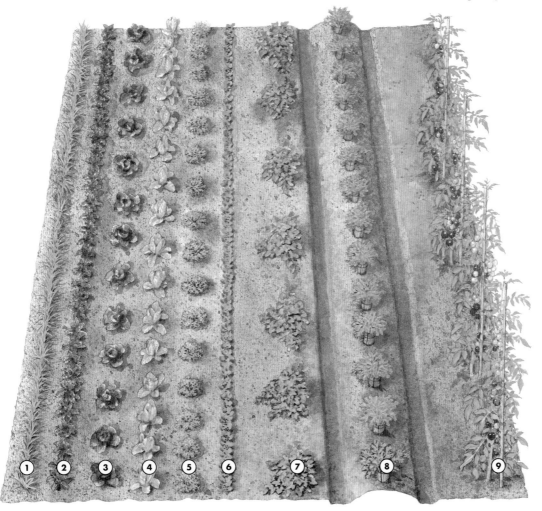

planting scheme
1 Spring onions
2 Beetroot
3 Radicchio
4 Cos lettuce
5 Salad bowl lettuce
6 Radish
7 Ridge cucumbers
8 Celery
9 Tomatoes
  (staked not bush)

a strawberry bed

Although strawberries are widely available from shops all year round, nothing tastes quite like those eaten straight from the plant. Strawberry plants are relatively cheap, easy to grow and look attractive whether in a bed or grown together in a container. With careful selection of varieties, they can be harvested from late spring right through to the autumn.

MATERIALS & EQUIPMENT

pegs and string

straw for mulching

posts, flower pots and netting

7 *Buxus sempervirens* 'Suffruticosa' per metre (3 ft) of hedging

5 strawberry plants per 2 m (6 ft) of strawberry row

2–3 buckets organic matter per square metre (yard)

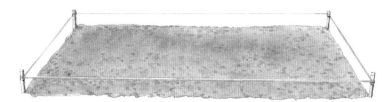

1   Mark out a plot using pegs and string, checking that the corners are right angles. An area of about 4.5 x 3 m (15 x 10 ft) will provide a generous crop.

2   Strawberry beds look attractive if they are surrounded by low hedges or raised boards. Plant young box, preferably a dwarf variety such as *Buxus sempervirens* 'Suffruticosa', in the spring at 150 mm (6 in) intervals around the bed. Pinch out the tips so that the plants bush out, which may take several years. Keep the box clipped back to the height and width required.

3   Prepare the ground thoroughly by removing all weeds and digging in plenty of well-rotted organic material. In late summer, buy plants that are guaranteed free from disease. Plant these at 400 mm (16 in) intervals in rows that are 600 mm (2 ft) apart. Water thoroughly; keep watered until they are established.

4   In the late spring, just as the fruit is beginning to swell, mulch underneath the plants with straw, tucking it up under their leaves and stems. This helps keep the fruit off the ground. Alternatively, black polythene can be placed under each plant.

board surround

A board surround to the strawberry bed not only looks good but is easier to prepare than a box hedge border. The bed can be built up by filling in with plenty of well-rotted compost and good quality loam, creating a fertile growing medium for the strawberries. The board edges also help to prevent straw in the bed from being blown or scattered.

pole fence surround

An alternative to a board surround is to use hazel or chestnut poles. These should be 25 mm (1 in) in diameter and split in half lengthways, then nailed to uprights that have been driven into the ground, or woven between them. Low woven hurdles can also be bought as ready-made panels.

5   Ripening fruits are a target for birds in late spring. To protect your strawberries, place short posts in the ground and drape netting over upturned flower pots – these allow the net to be moved without damaging the mesh. Weight the netting at the base.

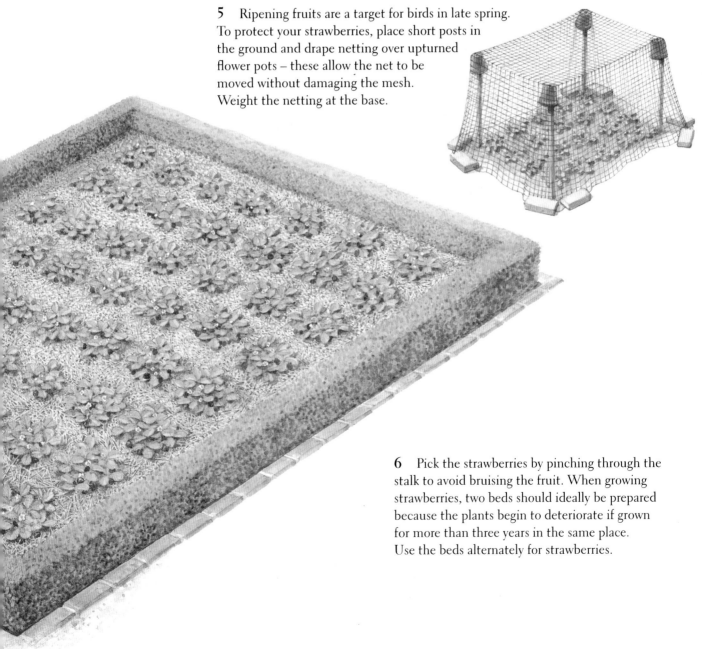

6   Pick the strawberries by pinching through the stalk to avoid bruising the fruit. When growing strawberries, two beds should ideally be prepared because the plants begin to deteriorate if grown for more than three years in the same place. Use the beds alternately for strawberries.

a taste of the orient

Traditionally, vegetable gardeners are a very conservative species, adopting new plants rather slowly. For example, it was several centuries after their introduction before potatoes and tomatoes were widely grown in Europe. But in recent times gardeners have become more adventurous, matching developments in the kitchen and restaurant by growing more and more exotic and oriental vegetables.

MATERIALS & EQUIPMENT

bricks • cement • concrete • hardcore

100 x 50 mm (4 x 2 in) wood for frame

25 x 25 mm (1 x 1 in) wood for battens

50 x 50 mm (2 x 2 in) wood for frames of lights

galvanized screws

glass cut to size • glazing sprigs and putty

wood preservative or paint

bricklayer's trowel and line • spirit level

saw and rebate saw or plane

pegs and string

seed and plants in variety (see page 231)

well-rotted organic material

1   Many oriental vegetables can be grown successfully under cover in a temperate climate. A cold frame built on a brick base provides a warm and permanent environment. To build the brick base, first use pegs and string to mark out a rectangular trench 2.1 x 1.5 m (6 ft 10 in x 5 ft) on its outer side, and 250 mm (10 in) wide. Dig down to a depth of 400 mm (16 in) and remove the soil.

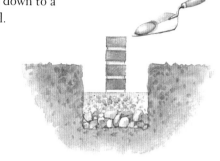

2   Ram 130 mm (5 in) of hardcore into the base of the trench; pour and level 100 mm (4 in) of concrete on top. Lay two courses of bricks below ground level.

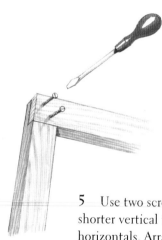

3   Build the rear wall so that the top is 600 mm (24 in) above ground level. The front wall should be 430 mm (17 in) above ground level. The side walls should slope between the two. The 'steps' in the top of the side walls can be filled with cement to create a smooth slope.

4   The top frame should be made from 100 x 50 mm (4 x 2 in) timber, cut to fit exactly the dimensions of the brick enclosure. Join the vertical and horizontal members by sawing out a section from each, half as deep as the timber itself, and as wide as the opposite member.

5   Use two screws to join the shorter vertical timbers to the longer horizontals. Arrange the screws on the diagonal – if they are in line, they are likely to split the wood.

6   Treat the frame with preservative, or paint it with primer, undercoat and topcoat. The frame can then be screwed onto the top of the brick enclosure.

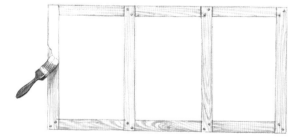

7   Nail wooden battens 25 x 25 mm (1 x 1 in) to the shorter cross-members. These will prevent the lights (the glazed panels of the cold frame) from sliding sideways when fitted later.

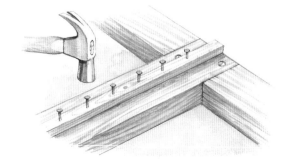

8   The simplest lights are rectangular wooden frames that hold a single sheet of glass. The three frames are made from 50 x 50 mm (2 x 2 in) wood, joined at the corners with halved joints, made as described in step 4. The frames should be just wide enough to fit snugly between the vertical battens of the frame – take your measurements carefully from the frame itself.

9   Using a rebate saw or plane, cut narrow ledges, or rebates, into the edges of the frame to hold the glass. Fit a sheet of horticultural-grade glass that has been cut to the correct size by a glazier. Secure using glazing sprigs and putty.

10   Dig the soil at the base of the enclosure, mixing in well-rotted organic material. If this soil is not particularly deep, good garden soil or potting compost can be added on top. Sow seed lengthways across the frame in shallow drills. Stagger the sowings so that crops mature at different times. Thin as necessary.

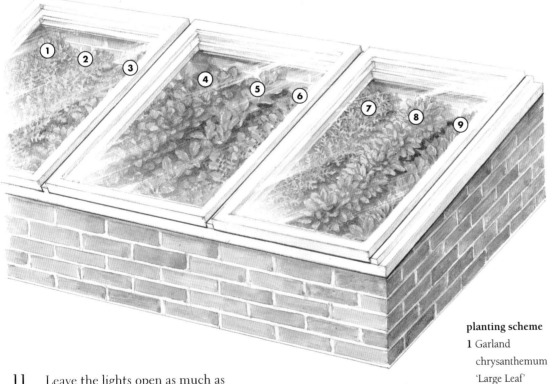

11   Leave the lights open as much as possible, but put them on to protect the crops during cold weather. The plants will need regular watering, especially around the edges where rain may not reach.

planting scheme
1 Garland
   chrysanthemum
   'Large Leaf'
2 Mustard greens
   'Southern Giant'
3 Mustard greens
   'Red Giant'
4 Pak choi 'Choki'
5 Japanese celery
6 Texsel greens
7 Garland
   chrysanthemum
   'Small Leaf'
8 Mustard greens
   'Green in the Snow'
9 Choy sum 'Purple
   Flowering'

herbs in a mixed border

Herb gardens need a lot of upkeep, and there are times of the year – especially from late summer onwards – when they begin to look a bit tired. One solution is to grow the herbs in a mixed border. When in season, the herbs add their fragrance and charm to the border; other plants take over when the herbs are not at their best. Another benefit is that herbs can be harvested when ready without leaving gaps in the garden.

MATERIALS & EQUIPMENT

pegs and string

100 x 10 mm (4 x ½ in) edging board

150 mm (6 in) pegs

stepping stones or broken slabs

gravel

sand

2.4 m x 300 mm (8 x 1 ft) heavy-duty polythene sheet

herbs and decorative plants in variety

well-rotted organic material

tamper

1 Draw an outline of your desired border, including access to all parts of the plot from a central gravel path and stepping stones. The stepping stones can be square, circular or irregular paving slabs; they do not need to be cemented in place and so can be moved if the planting is changed. The plot shown here is 2.4 m x 2.4 m (8 x 8 ft).

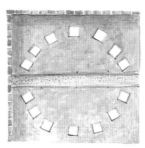

2 Use pegs and string to mark out the position of the path on the ground. Tamp down the soil firmly, so that the gravel will be almost flush to the ground when laid. Also tamp down the soil where the stepping stones are to be laid.

3 To prevent the gravel spilling into the border, construct a simple edging strip from lengths of 100 x 10 mm (4 x ½ in) treated timber. For every 900 mm (3 ft) of edging board, nail in a 150 mm (6 in) upright that has been sharpened to form a peg.

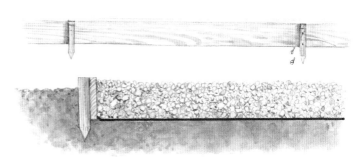

4 Gently hammer the pegs (and edging board) into the ground along the line of the path. Line the floor of the path with heavy-duty polythene before pouring in the gravel – this will help suppress weed growth. Fill the prepared path with a 100 mm (4 in) depth of gravel and rake the surface.

5 When laying the paving slabs, bed them onto a 50 mm (2 in) layer of sand to make them level.

6 Dig over the bed in autumn, removing any perennial weeds and adding well-rotted organic material. In spring, rake it through, removing any new weeds that have appeared. Place the plants, still in their pots, in position on the border. Stand back and envisage them in full growth, making any necessary adjustments to their positions.

Mix the plants so that the herbs are scattered throughout the border. This masks them during their less interesting phases and also means that you can savour their individual fragrances. Plant out starting from the back of the plot. Water well. Rake over the border to even the soil and remove footprints. If you intend to mulch, do so now.

7   The mint and the white willowherb are both runners and are best confined to prevent them spreading over the other plants. Small areas can be controlled by planting in a bottomless bucket. Larger confined areas can be created by digging a trench around the planting and inserting a vertical layer of thick polythene, at least 300 mm (12 in) deep.

planting scheme

1 *Philadelphus* 'Sybille' x 1

2 *Foeniculum vulgare* (fennel) x 3

3 *Lathyrus odoratus* (sweet pea) x 8

4 *Angelica archangelica* (angelica) x 1

5 *Oenothera biennis* (evening primrose) x 3

6 *Cynara cardunculus* (cardoon) x 1

7 *Satureja montana* (winter savory) x 1

8 *Petroselinum crispum* (parsley) x 5

9 *Borago officinalis* (borage) x 3

10 *Epilobium angustifolium* 'Album' (willowherb) x 3

11 *Mentha spicata* (mint) x 3

12 *Aster* x *frikartii* x 1

13 *Lavandula stoechas pendunculata* x 1

14 *Nepeta* x *faassennii* (catmint) x 2

15 *Allium tuberosum* (garlic chives) x 5

16 *Achillea millefolium* 'Cerise Queen' (yarrow) x 1

17 *Nepeta govaniana* x 3

18 *Lavandula angustifolia* (lavender) x 1

19 *Astrantia major* x 3

20 *Melissa officinalis* (lemon balm) x 1

21 *Laurus nobilis* (bay) x 2

22 *Thymus serpyllum* (thyme) x 3

23 *Nepeta sibirica* x 3

24 *Artemisia dracunculus* (French tarragon) x 3

25 *Origanum vulgare* (oregano) x 3

26 *Tanecetum parthenium* 'Aureum' x 2

27 *Ruta graveolens* (rue) x 1

28 *Calaminta grandiflora* (calamint) x 1

29 *Iris foetidissima* x 1

30 *Salvia officinalis* 'Icterina' (sage) x 1

31 *Levisticum officinale* (lovage) x 1

32 *Anemone* x *hybrida* x 3

33 *Allium schoenoprasum* (chives) x 5

34 *Myrrhis odorata* (sweet Cicely) x 1

35 *Rosmarinus officinalis* (rosemary) x 1

36 *Pelargonium graveolens* (scented geranium) x 3

37 *Geranium phaeum* x 1

38 *Dianthus* 'Miss Sinkins' x 3

39 *Alchemilla mollis* (lady's mantle) x 3

40 *Althaea officinalis* (marsh mallow) x 1

8   Draw up a complete planting plan. It is important not to underestimate the size to which some plants will grow. The plan is not sacrosanct and plants can change from year to year.

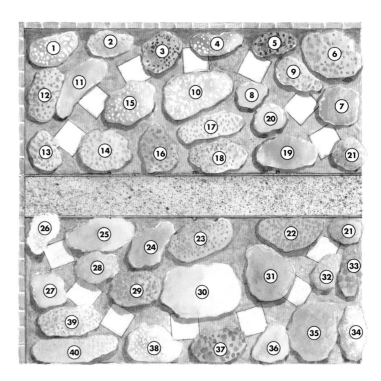

9   Herb gardens tend to become scruffy if not given regular attention. Deadhead flowering stems unless seed is required and remove all vegetation that is dying back or already dead.

a potager

A well-maintained vegetable garden is decorative in its own right, but a potager goes one step further because it is not only productive but also designed to look attractive. Creating a potager is basically a question of combining the colours, shapes and textures of plants in a well-considered layout. Paths, beds and ornamental structures can all play valuable roles. Such a garden may be a single bed or a combination of several.

MATERIALS & EQUIPMENT

terracotta pots

gravel

edging bricks

pegs and string

bottle and light-coloured sand

garden roller

vegetable seed and plants in variety

plenty of well-rotted organic material

1   Draw up a plan of your desired potager. In the first instance it should include only the bare bones and permanent features of the vegetable garden, including paths, edging and any hedges and trees.

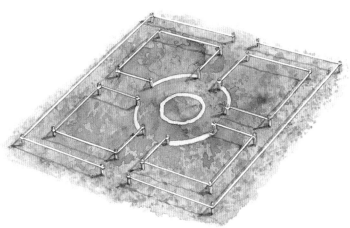

2   Thoroughly prepare the plot by removing all weeds and moving existing plants that are in the wrong place. Transfer your drawn plans to the ground using pegs and string. Curved lines may be laid out using lengths of flexible hose. Double-check all measurements – they must be right first time.

3   It is not essential to fix the paths permanently in concrete; indeed you may wish to enlarge or redesign the potager after a few years. Simply firm down the soil in the path areas with a garden roller and roll in several layers of gravel. Alternatively, lay paving slabs on a bed of sand. If using gravel, put the brick edging in place before laying the path.

4   Dig the bed areas, adding as much organic material as possible. Draw out the planting plan on each bed using a bottle of light-coloured sand as an oversized pencil. Sow the seed or set out the plants according to your needs. Planting a box hedge around the potager will give it a distinct boundary. Set out the young box plants at 150 mm (6 in) intervals (see page 226).

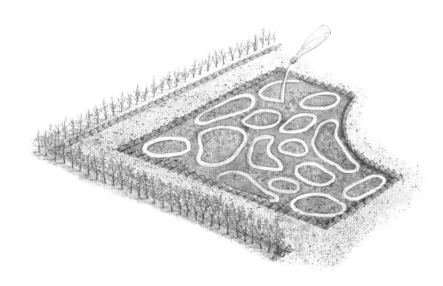

planting scheme
1 Sweet peas
2 Lavender
3 Alpine strawberries
4 Mizuma greens
5 Tarragon
6 Hyssop
7 French sorrel
   (in pots)
8 Lettuce in variety
9 Rhubarb
10 Florence fennel
11 Standard rose
12 Cardoons
13 Apple mint
14 Sage
15 Rosemary
16 Curly-leaved
   parsley
17 Squashes
18 Flat-leaved parsley
19 Ruby chard
20 Red atriplex
21 Bush tomatoes
22 Climbing rose
   ('Félicité Perpétue')
23 Chives
24 Leeks

5 Try to keep the potager looking its best throughout the summer. Harvesting plants leaves gaps that can upset the design, so keep a few young plants growing on in pots and trays to plant out as replacements. Quick-germinating, fast-growing crops, such as radishes, which can be sown in situ, can also be used as fillers.

filling gaps in the design
Terracotta pots can be planted up and placed either as a permanent part of the display or to fill a gap temporarily. Keep several pots in reserve to use whenever there is a blank space or to replace a pot that has finished.

a bean arbour

A seat beneath a flower-laden arbour is a feature associated with formal ornamental gardens, but there is no reason why such a decorative refuge cannot be incorporated into the kitchen garden. Covered with runner beans, the arbour can be both beautiful and productive. It is possible to create a permanent structure or something more temporary, which can be moved from one year to the next.

MATERIALS & EQUIPMENT

proprietary arbour framework

pegs and string

hardcore

treated edging boards 230 mm (9 in) wide, 20 mm (¾ in) deep

coarse gravel

sand

pea gravel

concrete

garden roller • tamper

4 scarlet runner bean plants, *Phaseolus coccineus*, per metre (3 ft)

well-rotted organic material

1 Choose an arbour frame from a garden centre or mail-order supplier, or find a blacksmith who will produce a more unusual design to your specifications. Think carefully about size – you may wish to fit a table as well as a bench under the arbour – and you should allow about 300 mm (12 in) for growth of the runner beans within the frame.

2 Clear the area of ground on which you want to place the arbour. Peg out the position of the arbour legs, and use further pegs and string to mark out the edges of a seating area and approaching path, both of which will be laid with gravel for durability.

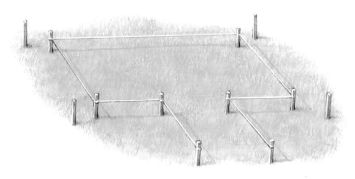

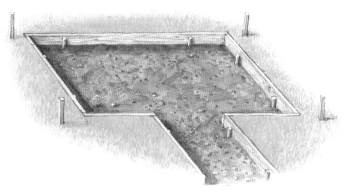

3 In the seating and path area, dig down to a depth of 200 mm (8 in) and remove the soil. Place treated boards around the dug area, securing with wooden pegs at 1 m (3 ft) intervals. Use a heavy roller to flatten the base.

4 Cover the base of the excavated area with hardcore to a depth of 100 mm (4 in). Lay a middle layer of coarse gravel and sand 5 cm (2 in) deep, and cover this with 25 mm (1 in) of pea gravel. Rake the surface to level off.

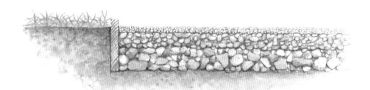

5 In sheltered sites, you don't need to concrete in the uprights of the arbour frame. Dig a hole for each post at least 450 mm (18 in) deep. Add a 100 mm (4 in) layer of gravel and place the framework in position. Refill the holes, ramming down the earth firmly with a tamper. In exposed sites, it is best to concrete the framework into position because wind pressure on the plant-covered arbour can be significant.

6 After the threat of frost has passed, dig the soil around the arbour and plant the runner beans. Plant a seedling against each post and then at 250 mm (10 in) intervals. Scatter slug pellets around the base. Water thoroughly.

7 Beans will naturally twine up and over the arbour but it may be necessary to direct them at the initial stages to ensure that there is even coverage. There is no need to tie the stems – it is enough just to tuck them in.

8 Don't let the beans dry out, especially once the flowers have started to form. To encourage bushier growth, pinch out the tops of the stems when they reach the middle of the arbour. The beans produce a display of red, pink or white flowers, depending on variety.

9 Pick the beans when about 150 mm (6 in) long. It is best to harvest every 3–4 days, taking the beans before their seeds swell. Don't leave old pods on the plants; they inhibit the formation of new ones.

tools and techniques

EQUIPMENT

For the gardener

Many of the projects in this book can be undertaken with the bare essentials of gardening equipment. Use a wheelbarrow for fetching and moving pots and mixing compost, and a sack truck for transporting larger containers. A stout cloth or purpose-made collecting cloth with handles saves mess when potting up and can be used to remove debris.

Indispensable hand tools include an old kitchen knife for weeding pots, a hand fork and trowel, a dibber to make holes for seeds or young plants, secateurs, sharp scissors, shears and a pruning saw. Old garden tools are often much nicer than new ones; buy them cheaply from a second-hand dealer. Failing that, invest in some stainless-steel tools, which wear well and are easy to clean.

For watering and spraying you need a watering can and a hosepipe. Use a hand-held spray for applying foliar feed and insecticide and a measuring jug for mixing them. Gardening can be a grubby business and harsh on the hands; use special tough gardening gloves for protection.

For the woodworker

There are no complicated procedures, joints or fixings in the construction projects described in this book. If you can cut a piece of wood and screw separate pieces together, you will be able to cope. When buying and cutting wood, use either metric or imperial measurements, depending on which system your supplier uses.

Use a handsaw (crosscut) for cutting timber and plywood to size. A workbench or pair of sawhorses are useful when cutting, although you can make do with a stout table. An electric jigsaw is quick and easy, particularly for curved cuts, but a coping saw will do.

The most versatile type of hammer is the claw hammer, which has one end for driving nails in and a curved claw for removing them. For drilling holes, use a metal brace with appropriate bits or the faster hand-held electric drill.

Most structures are secured with screws. A no. 2 screwdriver with a posidriv head is recommended for these projects. When inserting screws, use a bradawl to make a pilot hole; this marks the position and prevents the screwdriver from slipping and damaging the surface of the wood.

Other useful kit includes a pair of G-cramps for keeping work steady or holding pieces together and a smoothing plane.

For painting

Ordinary household paintbrushes are all that is required for most of the paintwork, but for decorative details an artist's brush will give more accuracy. Before you begin to paint, ensure that the surface is smooth and clean; a soft-bristled dusting brush works best. Use white spirit to clean the brushes.

Other general equipment that may be useful includes old rags and protective plastic sheets or paper. Exterior-grade wood filler can be used to fill cracks and indents and smoothed with sandpaper.

For metal projects

The metal constructions described in this book are relatively simple and need only a few special items of equipment, such as a pair of tinsnips for cutting lead facings and trimmings. A hacksaw is the best instrument for cutting thicker metals.

When shaping metal, use a vice on a bench together with a lump hammer to help to bend strips. For gilding, a range of metal and transfer leaves is available.

When handling lead, wear a pair of protective gloves.

WOODWORKING TECHNIQUES

Glues and fixings

The adhesive recommended for use in these projects is exterior-grade PVA (polyvinyl acetate) glue. Before gluing, always make sure that surfaces are free of dust and grease. Let the adhesive dry overnight to achieve its full strength.

Posidriv screws are the easiest screws to fix, especially when using an electric screwdriver. They are usually plated to protect them from rust, and come in a variety of sizes and types.

When screwing wood together, pre-drill one piece to fit the screw diameter and pilot drill the other. If you are using an electric screwdriver in softwood, a pilot hole may not be necessary.

To protect against rust, use sherardized pins and galvanized nails. Pins are often used with glue to reinforce a joint. For a neat finish, punch your pin below the surface and fill in the holes with a special wood filler.

Timber

Softwood has frequently been specified for use in the projects because it is inexpensive and easy to work. Before applying any other finish, treat it with a clear exterior-grade wood preservative.

Timber is available in sawn (rough) or planed (smooth) finishes. You need to tell your timber merchant which type you want because it affects the dimensions.

The final width and depth of a piece of planed timber will be about 3 to 5 mm ($\frac{1}{8}$ to $\frac{3}{16}$ in) less than the size quoted by a supplier. This is because a 50 x 25 mm (2 x 1 in) piece of sawn timber is the size you actually get, whereas in the case of planed timber the dimensions quoted reflect the size of the timber before it has been planed.

A sawn finish is generally preferable if you are using a decorative stain on your timber, because it gives the stain more of a key to the timber. A planed finish is more effective for a wood that is destined to be painted; such a finish is essential if you are intending to use gloss paint.

Plywood

Plywood is available in thicknesses from 3 mm ($\frac{1}{8}$ in) to 30 mm ($1\frac{3}{16}$ in). The cheapest exterior-grade plywood is shuttering ply. Also available is waterproof Far Eastern ply, which has a reddish tint (this can distort the colour of a stain finish), and marine ply, which is an expensive high-quality structural wood and is only worth using with hardwood.

Hardwood

Oak and teak are the best hardwood timbers for using outside, but they are expensive and hard to work. It is best to use a stained finish with oak and teak because it is difficult to make paint stay on them in the long term.

Preservatives

Unpreserved wood should be treated with anti-rot, anti-woodworm and fungicide; clear wood preservatives are available for this purpose. These are toxic to plants so they must be applied well in advance of planting.

Some preservatives are available specifically for horticultural work but many of them are tinted, which can affect the colour of a stain applied on top.

Stains

Some stains contain preservatives, others are only water-repellent. Stains tend to look better in muted colours and are affected by the colour of the wood to which you are applying them; they work most effectively on a sawn timber finish.

Paints

A wide range of paint types is available for exterior use on wood, including oil-based gloss, microporous exterior paint and ordinary exterior emulsion, which is long-lasting. Oil undercoat used on its own is good for a very flat finish.

Ordinary water-based paint is effective on terracotta, as is oil-bound or water-bound distemper, which can be used watered down to achieve a 'distressed' appearance. Concrete also takes emulsion paint or special exterior-grade masonry paint. For metal, use a gloss paint or a proprietary metal paint.

MAKING A BASIC WINDOW BOX

The instructions below explain how to make the basic structure for a herbal window box (pages 26–29), a raised scented window box (pages 34–37) or one of the balcony herb boxes (pages 38–41). Before embarking on one of these projects, refer to the appropriate list below to establish the quantities and types of wood that you will need. See the individual project for further decorative and planting advice.

Materials & equipment
• screwdriver
• electric drill with a 25 mm (1 in) flat bit or a brace and bit
• screws 40 mm (1½ in) long

For a herbal window box
• 4 sawn timber side boards, 250 x 150 x 25 mm (10 x 6 x 1 in)
• 4 sawn timber front and back boards, 780 x 150 x 30 mm (31 x 6 x 1 in)
• 4 sawn timber uprights, 300 x 30 x 30 mm (12 x 1¼ x 1¼ in)
• 2 sawn timber battens, 660 x 25 x 25 mm (26½ x 1 x 1 in)
• 2 sawn timber battens, 190 x 25 x 25 mm (7½ x 1 x 1 in)
• 1 piece of exterior-grade plywood, 715 x 245 x 10 mm (28¾ x 9¾ x ½ in)

For a raised scented window box
• 2 exterior-grade plywood side boards, 160 x 200 x 20 mm (6½ x 8 x ¾ in)
• 2 exterior-grade plywood front and back boards, 900 x 200 x 20 mm (36 x 8 x ¾ in)
• 2 sawn timber upright posts, 150 x 25 x 25 mm (6 x 1 x 1 in)
• 2 sawn timber battens, 810 x 25 x 25 mm (32½ x 1 x 1 in)
• 2 sawn timber battens, 110 x 25 x 25 mm (4½ x 1 x 1 in)
• 1 piece of exterior-grade plywood, 855 x 155 x 20 mm (34¼ x 6¼ x ¾ in)

For each balcony herb box
• 4 planed timber side boards, 200 x 100 x 25 mm (8 x 4 x 1 in)
• 4 planed timber front and back boards, 914 x 100 x 25 mm (36 x 4 x 1 in)
• 4 sawn timber upright posts, 150 x 25 x 25 mm (6 x 1 x 1 in)
• 2 sawn timber battens, 800 x 25 x 25 mm (32 x 1 x 1 in)
• 2 sawn timber battens, 150 x 25 x 25 mm (6 x 1 x 1 in)
• 1 piece of exterior-grade plywood, 850 x 200 x 25 mm (34 x 8 x 1 in)

1 Drill a hole in each corner of the side boards and screw the side boards to two of the upright posts. Fix the remaining side boards to the other two upright posts. Note that the raised scented box is composed of single plywood boards.

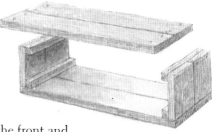

2 Pre-drill the front and back panels and screw them to the two side panels as shown, ensuring that the bottom panels are flush with the base of the upright posts. Turning the box on its side makes this step easier.

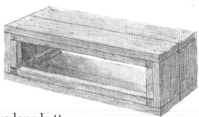

3 Screw the two long battens to the lower boards of the front and back panels from the inside so that they are flush with the base of the box. In the same way, screw the short support battens to the lower boards of the side panels.

4 Drill eight evenly spaced 25 mm (1 in) drainage holes in the piece of plywood. Cut a square notch from each corner of the base so that it fits around the upright posts, and slot into position on top of the support battens.

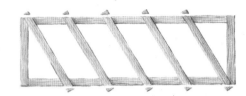

CUTTING MITRED CORNERS

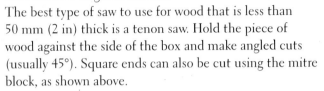

The most efficient way to cut a mitred joint in a piece of wood is to use a mitre block. This simple wooden jig has one raised side with slots cut in it to guide the saw.

The best type of saw to use for wood that is less than 50 mm (2 in) thick is a tenon saw. Hold the piece of wood against the side of the box and make angled cuts (usually 45°). Square ends can also be cut using the mitre block, as shown above.

MAKING A TRELLIS FENCE PANEL AND CORNER UNIT

Each corner unit of the trellis-enclosed herb garden on pages 116–19 consists of two trellis fence panels screwed to three corner posts. Use sawn timber – unless it has been pressure-treated, coat it with preservative.

Materials & equipment
For each panel
• 13 m x 50 x 25 mm (512 x 2 x 1 in) timber
• galvanized nails 25 mm (1 in) long

For each corner unit
• 3 pressure-treated posts, 900 x 80 x 80 mm (36 x 3 x 3 in)
• 3 metal post holders
• 2 pieces 80 x 25 mm (3 x 1 in) timber, each 1830 mm (74 in) long
• timber block for hammering post holders
• screws 80 mm (3 in) long
• sledgehammer
• galvanized nails 50 mm (2 in) long

1   From the 50 x 25 mm (2 x 1 in) timber, cut two lengths of 1830 mm (74 in) and two of 600 mm (24 in). On the longer pieces mark five equal sections with a pencil. Nail them to the uprights with the 25 mm (1 in) nails.

2   From the 50 x 25 mm (2 x 1 in) timber, cut five 790 mm (31½ in) pieces and nail them diagonally to the frame at the pencil marks. Cut off the pieces from the diagonals where they overlap the frame, as shown above.

3   From the 50 x 25 mm (2 x 1 in) timber, cut a further five 790 mm (31½ in) pieces and nail them to the frame in the same way, in the opposite direction. Cut off the excess wood. Make the second panel.

4   Place the timber block over each of the metal post holders and knock the holder into the ground so that the top of it protrudes only slightly above soil level.

5   Knock the two other holders into the ground in the same way, spaced at intervals of 1830 mm (74 in).

6   Knock each corner post into a post holder, as shown right.

7   Drill four holes in each of the panel uprights and then screw the uprights into the three posts using the 80 mm (3 in) screws.

8   To finish off, nail a 1830 mm (74 in) piece of 80 x 25 mm (3 x 1 in) capping to the top of each trellis panel.

SOLID BOUNDARIES

Many people regard brick and stone walls as the ultimate in boundaries. Although the materials are expensive, walls are long-lasting and provide an ideal home for many climbing and tender plants. Walls should be well made, so if you have any doubts about your ability to build a secure, safe structure, employ a professional builder. However, two or three courses of bricks or walls up to 450 mm (18 in) in height should be within the ability of most gardeners.

For most purposes, walls should be at least two bricks wide – that is, 230 mm (9 in) – although a single skin of bricks can be used for walls of only two or three courses. The pattern that bricks makes is important in regard to the strength of the wall as well as to its appearance.

Mixing concrete

Concrete that is ready to use can usually be bought only in large quantities, but it is simple to make. Concrete is a mixture of cement, coarse sand and aggregate, the last two usually being purchased ready mixed as 'ballast'.

For foundations, a mixture of one part cement to five parts ballast is needed. The precise measurements are not critical and the concrete is usually made in shovelfuls, one of cement to five of ballast.

The easiest way to mix concrete is to use a mechanical mixer. Add water a little at a time until the mixture is of the right consistency. Avoid making it too wet.

If you do not have access to a mixer, follow the step-by-step instructions for mixing concrete given below.

2   Slowly pour water into the hollow. It should not run out of the recess.

3   Mix the concrete and the water and add more water if necessary.

Brick bonds

The common bonds used in bricklaying are English bond and Flemish bond (both two bricks thick) and running bond (a single-brick thickness). Bricks laid front-on are described as stretchers. Bricks laid side-on are described as headers.

1   Mix the dry ingredients on a large sheet of board. Pile them into the centre of the board and create a hollow in the middle of the mixture.

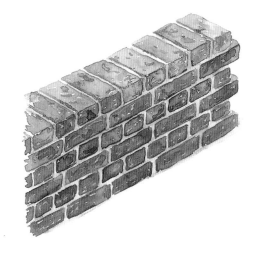

English bond

Two bricks deep, this bond comprises one, three or five courses of stretchers to one course of headers.

Flemish bond
Two bricks deep, this bond has one, three or five stretchers to one header per course.

Running bond
A single brick deep, this bond comprises only stretchers. These must be laid in a staggered formation to achieve maximum strength.

Checking level top and side
It is essential that walls are level in all directions, and a spirit level should be used repeatedly as a wall is built. Build the ends first and, using a line as a guide, build the centre one row at a time.

RAISED BEDS

Raised beds are particularly effective in small town gardens where they have been designed to complement the house. Such low structures are ideal for a novice builder.

Raised beds of brick, stone or concrete blocks require foundations. To provide drainage, leave gaps in the vertical pointing in the lower courses of the brickwork. A line of tiles towards the top will direct rainwater away from the brick surface. To prepare the bed, put a layer of broken rocks in the base and fill with good soil and organic material.

Foundations
Create foundations of hardcore and concrete, then build the raised bed one course at a time. Larger beds need a bond two bricks deep.

Drainage
Drainage is provided by means of broken stones in the base and grit added to the soil and well-rotted organic material.

Other materials
Railway sleepers do not need foundations. Lay them on a flat base and stagger the vertical joins, leaving small gaps for drainage.

SOIL PREPARATION

The most important aspect of creating a border is thorough preparation. Without it, even the best designs are likely to fail after a year or two, smothered by weeds or starved of nutrients and moisture.

Remove all perennial weeds before planting begins. Even a small piece of root will re-emerge as a weed, by which time it might be difficult to remove without digging out the whole border again. In lighter soils it may be possible to dig the soil and remove weeds at the same time, while on heavier soils it may be necessary to use a weedkiller; if so, always follow the directions on the packet. Dig the soil in the autumn and plant in the spring. This will allow any small piece of weed left in the soil to reveal itself so that it can be removed. In areas with warmer winters it is also possible to dig in spring and plant in autumn.

DOUBLE DIGGING

All borders should be dug over but they will be better, especially on heavy soils, if they are double dug (see below) so that the lower spit of earth is broken up. Do not dig if the soil is too wet. When the border is dug, incorporate as much well-rotted organic matter as possible into the lower

1 Dig a trench 300–450 mm (12–18 in) wide and 300 mm (12 in) deep. Reserve the removed earth.

2 Work the trench for a further 300 mm (12 in) and add organic matter. Dig out the next trench and use the earth to fill the first.

3 As before, work through the layer below, breaking up the ground with a fork and adding organic material.

4 When you reach the end of the border, fill the final trench with the reserved earth.

SOIL CONDITIONERS

Chipped or composted bark Best used as a mulch
Commercially prepared conditioners Good but expensive
Farmyard manure Good all-round conditioner as long as it does not contain weed seed
Garden compost Good all-round conditioner as long as it does not contain weed seed
Leaf mulch Excellent conditioner and mulch
Peat Little nutrient value and breaks down too quickly to be of great value
Seaweed Excellent conditioner, includes plenty of minerals
Spent hops Good conditioner but limited nutrients
Spent mushroom compost Good conditioner and mulch; includes lime

spit. This improves the structure of the soil and provides nutrients for the plants. Its fibrous nature also helps to preserve moisture deep in the soil where the plants' roots need it. Once the soil has been dug over, leave it for several months. This will allow the rain and frost to break it down and kill any pests. Residual weeds will also reappear. Avoid walking on the area while it is weathering.

GARDEN COMPOST

One of the best ways of providing organic material for the garden is to make your own compost. Almost any plant material can be used as long as it is not too woody and does not contain weed seeds. Avoid diseased material and virulent weeds; uncooked vegetable waste is recommended.

Place all the material in a container that has air holes in the sides. Avoid creating too thick a layer of any one material, such as grass cuttings. Keep the bin moist but covered so that the compost retains heat and to prevent it becoming too wet and chilled in heavy rain. Turn the heap occasionally.

If possible, have two bins, one for collecting material; three allows a bin for rotting down.

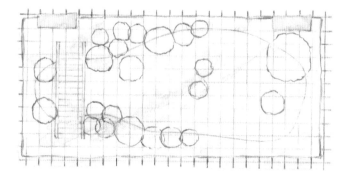

PLANNING A BORDER

Before you draw up a plan for a border, decide what you are aiming to achieve. For example, you may want a low-maintenance border, a bright, vibrant border or a romantic display in pastel tones. Is it more important to you to create dramatic effects with foliage or to have plenty of flowers for cutting?

Consider also the position of the border and its physical attributes. Does it get plenty of sun or is it in perpetual shade? Is the soil acid or alkaline? Is it wet or dry or just about right? Is it heavy or sandy? All these factors have a bearing on how much work you will have to put in and on what plants you can and cannot grow. For example, if you live in an area where there is chalky soil, you will not be able to grow rhododendrons.

Then decide what plants you want to use to create the desired effect. This is best done over at least one season so that you can go round gardens, notebook in hand, compiling a list of desirable plants. Looking through books is also another stimulating source of ideas. After you have compiled an initial list, the next stage is to find out whether your preferred plants can be obtained locally or if tracking them down will involve a long search. Adjust your list accordingly.

You are now ready to plot the planting. Using squared paper, draw out the border to scale and then mark out the plants in position, sketching them at their eventual spread (above). You do not need to be good at drawing to produce a useful plan. Adjacent colours should be sympathetic and the border should have an even spread of interest throughout the year. It is a good idea to draw the bed at different seasons so that you can assess how successful the plan will be through the year, and from the front to compare the plants' relative heights. If problems appear as you are making the sketches, it is much easier to put them right at this stage than it would be after planting.

PLANTING

Rake or lightly fork over the soil, removing any weeds that have appeared. If only a small amount of organic material was added when the soil was being prepared, a light dressing of a general fertilizer can be raked into the surface. Follow the directions on the packet.

The best time for planting shrubs and trees is from late autumn to early spring, and for perennials it is either autumn or spring. Annuals should not be planted out until the threat of frost is past if they are tender, or in autumn or spring if they are hardy. To get an idea of how the display will look, position the plants, still in their pots, in the border and make any necessary adjustments.

Dig a hole wider than each plant's root ball and insert the plant so that it is at the same depth as it was in its pot or, if it is bare-rooted, in its previous bed. If the roots have become pot-bound or tangled, gently tease them out and spread them in the hole. Fill the hole and firm the soil around the roots. When planting a tree or a shrub, dig a much larger hole than the plant's root ball and dig plenty of well-rotted organic material into the bottom of the hole. Mix some into the soil that will go back into the hole once the plant is in place.

If staking the tree or shrub, position the stake before planting so that the roots will not be damaged by the stake driving through them.

USING A MULCH

Once all the plants are in the bed, water them thoroughly, rake over the surface to level it off and apply a mulch.

Mulches cover the surface of the soil, helping to keep moisture in and preventing weed seed from germinating; they can also create an attractive background for plants.

Organic mulches consist of chipped bark, leaf mould, spent mushroom compost or even grass cuttings and straw. Inorganic mulches include plastic sheeting (which should be covered with soil, gravel or other stones), gravel or pebbles.

SOWING SEED

Direct sowing: annuals
If clumps of plants are required, mark out the ground with fine sand before sowing.

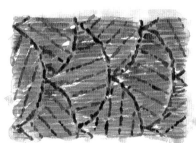

Direct sowing: perennials
1   Dig the soil well, then rake it over to produce a fine tilth for sowing.

2   Make a shallow drill with the edge of a hoe, using a guide line if necessary. This can be made using pegs and a length of string.

3   Pour some water into the drill. This will help to consolidate the hollow and will ensure the seeds receive adequate moisture.

4   Sow the seed, sprinkling a fine line into the drill. Do not overfill – overcrowding can starve seedlings of nourishment.

5   Draw the soil back into the drill with the back of the rake and lightly water in.

Direct sowing
If sowing annuals into a border, break down the dug soil into a fine tilth with a rake. If several clumps of plants are required, mark out each area with some sand so that it is easy to see where to sow. Scatter the seed over the required area; gently rake them in. Water with a fine-rosed watering can.

If sowing perennials in a seed bed, draw out a shallow drill with the edge of a hoe, using a guide line if necessary. Pour a little water into the drill and scatter seed along it. Draw the soil back into the drill and water.

Pot sowing

If only a few plants are required, or if it is necessary to sow the seed in gentle heat, they should be sown in a tray or pot. Using a good seed compost, fill the pot and tap it on the bench to settle the contents; level and lightly press it down. Sow the seed thinly and cover with a layer of fine grit or compost. Water the compost carefully. Many annuals need to be placed in a warm environment such as a propagator or heated greenhouse but perennials rarely require heat and can be kept outside in a sheltered position. Keep moist until the seeds germinate and then prick out into trays or individual pots. Tender seedlings that have been sheltered should be hardened off in a cold frame before planting out after the threat of frost has passed.

Sowing in a pot
Once seeds have been sprinkled in a pot, cover with compost or a fine grit as recommended for the particular plant.

Planting in a tray
Once seedlings have grown they should be pricked out carefully and planted on in individual pots to continue growing.

Planting bulbs

As a general guide, make sure the planting hole for a bulb is at least three times as deep as the bulb is tall.

always be bought in the green, while cyclamen are best bought as potted specimens. Some plants can be relied upon to increase with little attention. These are often naturalized bulbs, those that have been left to grow in grass or under trees. If they become congested after a few years, lift and replant.

BUYING PLANTS

Garden centres sell a reasonably extensive range of plants, but specialist nurseries have a much larger selection, including unusual plants.

Many nurseries also send plants by mail order, which is a great advantage if they are some distance away. Order early because demand can outstrip supply for many catalogue plants, and inform the nursery if you expect to be away when the plants are due to arrive – otherwise you might come home to a box of dead plants.

When buying plants, do not always go for the largest specimen. A medium-sized plant free from pests and diseases is best. Avoid a plant that is pot-bound (below).

The alternative to buying plants is to grow your own from seed, by division or from cuttings. This is a much cheaper approach but plants will need time to mature. Rare plants are often available only as seed.

BULBS

Plant spring-flowering bulbs in autumn, and summer- and autumn-flowering bulbs in spring. The depth of the planting hole should be at least three times the height of the bulb. While daffodils, tulips and several other bulbs can be bought as dry specimens, it is better to buy others either 'in the green' – freshly dug with their leaves still green – or growing in pots. For example, snowdrops should

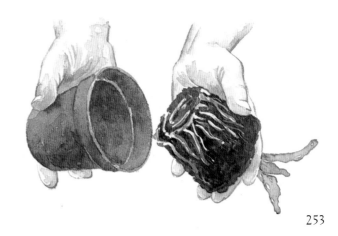

care and maintenance

CHOOSING A CONTAINER

When deciding what sort of containers would be most appropriate for your garden, you can either start by choosing the plants and find containers suited to the nature and habit of the plants, or start with the containers and devise planting schemes to suit them. The latter approach may have the advantages that the containers will be there all year round and will have to fit in with the character and scale of the setting.

Consider where in the garden you need plant interest and what sort of container would look good in that position. To be appreciated from a distance, the container needs to be bold and simple in outline. The height of the planting must also be decided in relation to the rest of the garden; generally, the taller the planting the larger the container needed.

Elaborate detail is best in a foreground position where it can be seen clearly, and the same applies to planting – complex schemes using delicate plants are best seen close to, where their detail can be fully appreciated.

The colour of your material should be chosen to harmonize with the house and the rest of the garden as well as with the intended planting scheme. As a general rule, materials that weather and patinate are more appealing; hand-thrown terracotta patinates the quickest. Lead, stone and cast stone also patinate with age, and the process can be speeded up by applying vinegar in the case of lead, and yoghurt, milk or liquid manure in the case of stone and cast stone. One way to age a pot quickly is to place it under the drip of trees.

Cast iron and wood both need to be painted or stained to preserve them. Use a faded blue-grey-green, referred to as 'Versailles blue', a colour often seen on the shutters of old houses in Italy and France.

LOOKING AFTER CONTAINERS

Containers need to be scrupulously cleaned and scrubbed before planting; scrub them well on the inside with clean water but try to preserve the patina on the outside. Some containers are best used with plastic liners, especially if you change your schemes with the seasons. Plastic liners are particularly useful for large Versailles cases and urns. Check that your terracotta is frostproof if you are going to leave it outside all year round. In winter even hardy plants in pots will need their roots protecting against severe frost – wrap the pot with hessian (as shown below left), straw or bubble wrap. Where plants are in liners, pack straw between the plastic pot and container for protection. In early autumn or spring, examine the condition of your containers and repaint them if necessary.

All containers need good drainage. Ensure that there are enough holes to let out excess moisture and put a thin layer of pot shards or gravel on the base of pots.

PLANTING MEDIUM

Different plants need different composts. For semi-permanent plantings use an aerated nutritious compost, and for short-term schemes a soil-less multi-purpose compost. Some plants have specific needs. For instance, special composts are available for bulbs, and very gritty free-draining soil-based composts are recommended for some alpine and rock plants. John Innes composts are numbered 1, 2 and 3 according to their nutritional content. Note whether your plant needs a fast- or slow-growing medium.

Peat-based mixtures are appropriate for containers because they are light, but they also have a tendency to dry out, so are unsuitable for plants that are difficult to water. Loam-based mixtures offer a more stable alternative but carry more weight. Also available are bark, coir and wood-fibre composts that work well in containers.

POTTING PLANTS

The size of the pot should complement the size of the planting and needs to be large enough to contain the root ball and sustain growth. Some plants dislike being repotted repeatedly and do not mind being root-bound, whereas others need to be regularly potted on as they grow. Most seasonal plantings, if properly fed and watered, can stand being in a confined pot.

For a shrub or tree, start off with a large container that will support its growth for a number of years before the inevitable repotting. Some Versailles cases are specifically designed for ease of repotting; the sides let down for easy removal of the root ball. Such a design might be suitable for large plants such as orange and lemon trees, camellias and greenhouse exotics.

When potting up a multiple seasonal planting, you may need to cram in the depotted root balls to create the desired effect. This would not be appropriate for permanent plantings but in this case, as long as the roots have space to develop downwards, the plants will survive.

For permanent plantings, take extra care with root ball placement. Single specimens should be placed centrally in the pot and firmed down. Make sure the soil surface is at least 25 mm (1 in) below the top edge of the pot so that there is space for a water reservoir. In the case of standards, choose a specimen with an upright and secure stem (stake if required), because it is hard to correct this later.

Climbing plants can have supports fixed in the soil or to the container – there is a wide range of stakes, metal shapes, and trellis obelisks available, which you can construct yourself or buy ready-made.

WATERING

In summer, the key to successful container gardening is regular watering. Small pots, particularly those made of terracotta, dry out very quickly, and during spells of hot weather they will need watering twice a day – in the early morning and in the evening, to avoid sunburn to wet leaves. Water larger pots only once a day. Always soak the plant thoroughly by filling the reservoir at the top up to the brim. If you use a hose, use one with a rose end so that the water pressure does not wash away any compost.

Reduce watering as the growing season ends. In winter most plants need only to be kept from drying out, so check them every few days to make sure they are still moist. Some plants that are dormant in winter prefer the soil to be almost dry – check individual plants for special needs. A useful way to conserve moisture is to place a layer of mulch over the soil.

FEEDING

There are various methods for feeding pot-grown plants. Slow-release granules are good for long-term plantings – sprinkle them onto the surface of the soil and rake them into the compost. Other chemical feeds can be mixed into the compost when planting. Liquid feeds are diluted in water and used as part of the watering regime. Foliar feeds are sprayed on for instant effect, and organic material can be used as a top dressing. Use homemade compost, well-rotted manure or blood and bone, applied during the growing season.

When planting, always follow the specific feed requirements because some plants like a relatively impoverished soil and do not respond well to overfeeding.

PESTS AND DISEASES

Plants that are stressed as a consequence of poor watering and feeding are more vulnerable to attack – so the surest way to prevent the invasion of pests and diseases is to take the best possible care of your plants and containers. Cleanliness of pots and tools helps to keep bacterial diseases at bay, as does keeping a regular eye on their health.

Plants are vulnerable to three groups of diseases: bacterial, fungal and viral. Viral diseases are untreatable – destruction of the plant is the only remedy.

Below is a typical example of bacterial leaf spot (left) and powdery mildew (right). Benomyl is the most useful spray for bacterial leaf spot, black spot, fungal leaf spot and powdery mildew; spray only on calm days after sunset so as not to harm beneficial insects.

The most common pests to attack container plants are aphids (greenfly and blackfly); these can be sprayed with pirimicarb. Whitefly can be treated with permethrin, and scale insects with a mixture of liquid paraffin and nicotine.

Always take care to store garden sprays and chemicals well out of the reach of children and pets – and wear gloves and a mask as directed.

MAINTAINING BORDERS

Staking, deadheading, regular watering and weeding all contribute to a thriving border.

Pea-stick supports
These are versatile, flexible supports that can be drawn together and tied to form a supporting case around vulnerable plants.

Netting support
A net support is a permanent device. The plant grows up and through the mesh which, in time, will be hidden by foliage.

String and stakes
Stakes with a network of strings are useful as a temporary support for larger, spreading shrubs until they are established.

Staking
Plants that could blow over or become top-heavy in rain need to be staked. Support tall flower spikes, such as delphiniums, with individual canes; clumps can be held by pea-sticks, netting supported between posts or by proprietary linking stakes. Stake the plants when they are half-grown.

Trees and shrubs should be staked with a single or double stake. For most trees it is enough to use a single tie low down, 300 mm (12 in) from the ground. For standards and spindly trees use a taller stake and two ties.

Staking trees
A single tie should be placed low down to support a tree. This will give sufficient extra stabilty until the tree is established.

Staking standard bushes
Standards need a taller stake than most trees and two ties (the first tie is shown here, positioned high up the stem).

Deadheading
Unless you want to collect the seed or save the seed-heads for decoration, cut off any dead or dying flowers. Many perennials, including nepeta, several geraniums, alchemilla and oriental poppies, should be cut to the ground after flowering; this will encourage the growth of a fresh crop of leaves, and the plant will then be useful for foliage effect.

Watering
Water plants in dry conditions, ensuring that they get a thorough soaking, the equivalent of at least 25 mm (1 in) across the surface. Do not water in full sun. Feeding should not be necessary if the border is top dressed regularly. In autumn fork in the organic mulch and replace it with a

layer of farmyard manure or garden compost. Dig this into the bed in spring and reapply the usual mulch.

Weeding

Remove any weeds on sight. Regular checks will keep weeds under control; if left, they can be hard to eradicate. With conscientious application, it should be possible to hand-weed a border. Avoid using chemical herbicides on a planted area.

Autumn care

Cut back most perennials in autumn. This task can be left till spring so that the old stems give some protection to the crown from frosts, but tidying during the dormant season means there is less to do in the spring rush.

PRUNING

Ornamental trees and evergreen shrubs generally do not need pruning, except to remove any dead or dying branches, although you may want to remove stems for aesthetic reasons. By contrast, most deciduous shrubs benefit from regular attention. The aim is to keep the bush healthy and vigorous so that it produces good foliage and

flowers. To do this, up to a third of the old wood should be cut out each year, encouraging new growth. As a general rule, the best time to prune is immediately after the bush has finished flowering. Diseased, dead or weak growth should also be removed. Pruning cuts should be sloping, just above a viable bud.

Pruning and maintaining climbers

Twining plants and plants that produce tendrils, such as honeysuckle and clematis, do best with wirework support or trellis, or climbing over another plant. Clinging climbers such as ivy need no additional support. The sheer weight of an untended climber can damage a support, while overcrowding can adversely affect flower production. Pruning ensures an attractive framework and promotes vigorous growth and plentiful flowers.

Roses

Climbing and rambling roses can be very vigorous and need to be tied to a structure. They create excellent cover but benefit enormously from pruning and training. Climbing roses can be pruned in autumn or winter, while rambling roses should be pruned after flowering, in late summer. Deadheading assists growth but should not be carried out if you want hips.

Pruning a climbing rose
Do not prune during the first year. After that, only prune main shoots if they grow beyond their allotted space, but prune side shoots by two-thirds.

Pruning a rambling rose
Do not prune in the first year. Then remove two or three whole stems each year (this is easier done in sections); cut back the remaining main stems by a third and side shoots by two-thirds.

Clematis

Pruning clematis can be rather complicated because different varieties of the plant need to be treated in different ways.

There are three groups of clematis, and it is essential to know to which group a specimen belongs to avoid destructive or insufficient pruning. Examples of clematis varieties and their groups are given below. Plants belonging to the first group should be pruned in autumn, while plants in the other two groups should be pruned in early spring. Correct pruning will encourage full growth and maximum flowering.

Clematis group 1

Early-flowering species that flower on the previous year's shoots: only prune out dead material. If you want to prevent the plant from becoming too large and heavy, remove a few stems each year.

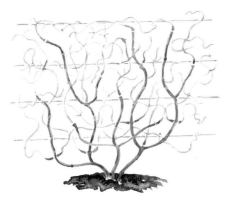

Clematis group 2

Large-flowered varieties that flower early to mid-season on new shoots from the previous year's stems: prune old wood lightly.

Clematis group 3

Large-flowered varieties that flower late on new wood: these can be cut right back to just above a strong pair of buds.

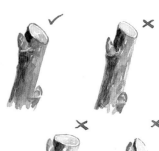
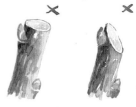

Pruning cuts

Correct cuts are very important to the health of all plants. Cuts should be sloping, just above a viable bud (top left).

EXAMPLES OF CLEMATIS

C. 'Abundance' 3	C. 'Little Nell' 3
C. alpina 1	C. macropetala 1
C. armandii 1	C. 'Marie Boisselot' 2
C. 'Barbara Dibley' 2	C. 'Miss Bateman' 2
C. 'Barbara Jackman' 2	C. montana 1
C. 'Bill MacKenzie' 3	C. 'Mrs Cholmondeley' 2
C. cirrhosa 1	C. 'Nelly Moser' 2
C. 'Comtesse de Bouchaud' 3	C. 'Niobe' 2
C. 'Countess of Lovelace' 2	C. 'Perle d'Azur' 3
C. 'Daniel Deronda' 2	C. 'Rouge Cardinal' 3
C. 'Doctor Ruppel' 2	C. 'Royal Velours' 3
C. 'Duchess of Albany' 3	C. 'Star of India' 2
C. 'Elsa Späth' 2	C. tangutica 3
C. 'Ernest Markham' 2	C. 'The President' 2
C. 'Etoile Violette' 3	C. tibetana 3
C. 'Gipsy Queen' 3	C. 'Ville de Lyon' 3
C. 'Hagley Hybrid' 3	C. viticella 3
C. 'H. F. Young' 2	C. 'Vyvyan Pennell' 2
C. 'Jackmanii' 3	C. 'W. E. Gladstone' 2
C. 'Lasurstern' 2	

Wisteria

Wisteria needs to be pruned twice a year, once immediately after flowering and again in winter. Wisteria that has been allowed to run free without any pruning soon runs out of flower-power. In late summer, cut back all the new growth to four or five leaves. If you want to extend the plant's coverage, leave a few shoots to grow on. In winter, reduce the stems even further.

Late summer

Cut back all the new growth to 150 mm (6 in), or four or five leaves.

Winter

Cut back the stems even further, to 80–100 mm (3–4 in), or two to three buds.

Other climbers

A simple pruning regime can make all the difference to the performance of a climber, but it is vital to know if the plant flowers on old or new wood. Follow these guidelines: remove all dead, diseased and dying wood; cut out a few of the older stems to promote new, vigorous growth; do not allow plants to become tangled. Climbers that flower on old wood should be pruned immediately after flowering; those that flower on new wood should be left until late winter or spring.

Plants that flower on new wood

Plants that flower on fresh growth should be pruned in late winter or early spring.

Plants that flower on old wood

These plants need pruning straight after flowering so that they have time to produce new shoots before winter.

Ways of fixing plants to structures

A variety of devices and structures can be attached to walls and fences to give plants support. Wires can be discreet, wooden trellis decorative and, for smaller areas and plants that produce good leaf-cover, a rigid plastic mesh is effective (but unattractive, which is why it needs to be hidden).

For trellis, screw battens or blocks to the wall or fence (first drill holes into a wall with a masonry bit and use a plastic or wooden plug); these will make it easier to weave stems behind the trellis and to tie them in.

Plastic mesh is attached using proprietary clips that are screwed or nailed in place. The mesh can be unclipped to help pruning or maintenance of the supporting structure.

A YEAR IN THE HERB GARDEN

The ideal time to plan the year ahead in your herb garden is at the end of the growing season because – except in years when heavy frosts occur – mid-autumn is the best time of year to start planting herbs.

Mid-autumn
● Container-grown plants can be planted at any time of year but they will become established much better if they are planted in autumn or spring. Water the plant well in its pot before planting. If you have a dry bare-rooted plant, plunge the root ball into a bucket of water first.
● If you are planting a new herb bed on uncultivated ground, prepare the soil as described in Double Digging (page 250).
● Plant trees, shrubs and hardy herbaceous herbs. Check how far apart they need to be planted based on their ultimate spread, and, depending on the space available, plant in groups of three, five or seven.
● To prevent invasive herbs such as mint from taking over, plant them in a plastic bucket or other container, which should then be sunk into the ground.
● Move tender herbs in containers into a greenhouse or conservatory.
● Grow parsley and marjoram in pots and overwinter under glass for a winter supply.
● Cut back larger shrubs.

Late autumn
● Continue to plant bare-rooted trees and shrubs while the ground is frost-free. Plant low edging such as box, hyssop, rue and lavender about 230 mm (9 in) apart.
● Cover tender herbs ready for winter.

Early winter
● Remove soggy herbaceous and annual growth as the herbs die back but leave other growth in place to provide winter protection for smaller plants.
● Keep the herb garden neat, as you would in summer.

Midwinter
● Now is a good time to think about next year's planting. Order your seeds and plan alterations or improvements.

Late winter
● Towards the end of the season sow the seed of tender herbs indoors.
● Plant pot-grown hardy herbaceous herbs and shrubs in frost-free weather.

Early spring
● Clear away all dead or herbaceous growth.
● Add a dressing of bonemeal to the ground and fork over the soil.
● Make the first seed sowing of hardy annuals and biennials in the ground if it is not too wet.
● Continue to plant hardy pot-grown herbs in frost-free weather.

Mid-spring
● Plant container-grown herbs if required.
● Cut back shrubs such as lavender, sage and santolina to keep them compact.
● Prune larger shrubs to shape.
● Continue to sow seed outdoors and to plant container-grown herbs.
● An annual spring mulch of homemade compost or other organic fertilizer for your herbs would be beneficial.

- Cut back Mediterranean shrubs such as rosemary and lavender to encourge compact new growth.
- Pinch out the growing ends of young shrubs to create a neat shape if required.

Late spring
- Move half-hardy and tender plants to a sheltered place so that they can be hardened off for an early summer planting.
- Beware of late frosts.
- Weed from mid-spring to early summer.
- Stake and support any trailing plants.

Early summer
- This is perhaps the best season in the herb garden, with the foliage looking fresh and green. Many herbs will now be ready for harvesting.
- Trim dwarf hedges and formal plantings.

Midsummer
- Collect seed from early annuals and biennials for autumn or spring sowing and carefully label in separate envelopes.
- Harvest plants for drying and preserving.
- Collect rose petals and lavender flowers for pot-pourri and sachets.

Late summer
- Continue to collect petals and scented leaves from plants such as lemon verbena and scented geraniums, and harvest herbs for drying and preserving.
- Collect seed as it ripens.
- Continue to trim formal hedges.

Early autumn
- Dig up tender and half-hardy plants and overwinter in pots under glass or inside.
- Fork over the soil and fertilize any permanent planting.

Harvesting and drying
Harvest herbs on a dry, sunny morning after any moisture has evaporated from the leaves but before they are exposed to full sun. Handle aromatic herbs as little as possible to avoid bruising them and releasing the volatile oils. Foliage is usually harvested just before the flowers appear.

Small-leaved herbs should be dried in small bunches on the stem. Leaves should then be removed from the stem and stored in sealed containers. Dry whole flowers off the stalk, face upwards on a tray lined with paper.

HERBS IN CONTAINERS

Growing in containers allows you to position culinary herbs conveniently near the kitchen door so that you can harvest your herbs when required. Growing tender herbs such as basil in containers means that they can conveniently be moved under glass or into a conservatory to overwinter.

You can also control the soil and growing conditions in a container far more easily than you can in a garden. Depending on the requirements of a particular herb, you can provide, for example, sharp-draining sandy soil or moist peaty soil. Many herbs enjoy the free-draining dryish conditions that can be created by container culture.

Planting containers
When planting up your containers, make sure that the planting medium is suited to the type of herb. In a mixed planting, it is important to consider how large the herbs will eventually get and whether some may overwhelm others, although this can be corrected with pruning and annual division.

Check the moisture level of the soil in the containers on a daily basis and water every day. Water thoroughly from late spring throughout the growing season. The best time to water pot-grown herbs is in the early morning or in the evening. Make sure there is at least 25 mm (1 in) between the top of the compost and the pot in order to provide a watering reservoir. Feed the herb with a liquid fertilizer at least once every two weeks during the growing season.

If your herbs become pot-bound – with their roots protruding from the base of the container – repot in spring. Either replant in a larger pot or simply divide the plant and repot into two or more pots.

useful addresses

GARDEN CENTRES AND NURSERIES

Beth Chatto Gardens
Elmstead Market
Colchester
Essex CO7 7DB
01206 822007
www.bethchatto.co.uk

Blooms of Bressingham
Bressingham
Diss
Norfolk IP22 2AB
01379 688585
www.bloomsofbressingham.co.uk

Burncoose Nurseries
Gwennap
Redruth
Cornwall TR16 6BJ
01209 860316
www.burncoose.co.uk

Capital Gardens
Alexandra Palace
London N22 4BB
020 8444 2555
www.capitalgardens.co.uk

Clifton Nurseries
5A Clifton Villas
London W9 2PH
020 7289 6851
www.clifton.co.uk

Notcutts Garden Centres
Woodbridge
Suffolk IP12 4AF
01394 383344
www.notcutts.co.uk

Pottertons Nursery
Moortown Road
Nettleton
Caistor
Lincolnshire LN7 6HX
01472 851714
www.pottertons.co.uk

River Garden Nurseries
Troutbeck
Otford
Sevenoaks
Kent TN14 5PH
01959 525588
www.river-garden.co.uk

The Romantic Garden Nursery
The Street
Swannington
Norwich
Norfolk NR9 5NW
01603 261488
www.romantic-garden-nursery.co.uk

Stapeley Water Gardens
London Road
Stapeley
Nantwich
Cheshire CW5 7LH
01270 623868
www.stapeleywg.com

SPECIALIST PLANT SUPPLIERS
Bulbs

Avon Bulbs
Burnt House Farm
Mid Lambrook
South Petherton
Somerset TA13 5HE
01460 242177
www.avonbulbs.com

De Jager & Sons
The Nurseries
Staplehurst Road
Marden
Kent TN12 9BP
01622 831235
www.dejagerflowerbulbs.co.uk

Jacques Amand
The Nurseries
Clamp Hill
Stanmore
Middlesex HA7 3JS
020 8420 7110
www.jacquesamand.com

Climbing plants

TH Barker & Son
Baines Paddock Nursery
Haverthwaite, Ulverston
Cumbria LA12 8PF
015395 58236
www.ukclematis.co.uk

J. Bradshaw and Son
Busheyfield Nursery
Herne Bay
Kent CT6 7LJ
01227 375415

Foliage plants

The Fern Nursery
Grimsby Road
Binbrook
Lincolnshire LN8 6DH
01472 398092
www.fernnursery.co.uk

Goldbrook Plants
Eye
Hoxne
Suffolk IP21 5AN
01379 668770

Halecat Garden Nursery
The Yard
1 Halecat Cottages
Witherslack
Cumbria LA11 6RT
01539 552536
www.halecat.co.uk

Hoecroft Plants (grasses)
Severals Grange
Holt Road
Wood Norton
Dereham
Norfolk NR20 5BL
01362 684206
www.hoecroft.co.uk

Herbaceous perennials

Cally Gardens
Gatehouse of Fleet
Castle Douglas
Scotland DG7 2DJ
Information: 01557 815029
www.callygardens.co.uk

Four Seasons Perennials
Forncett St. Mary
Norwich
Norfolk NR16 IJT
01508 488344
www.fsperennials.co.uk

Hadspen Garden & Nursery
Castle Cary
Somerset BA7 7NG
01749 813707
www.hadspengarden.freeserve.co.uk

Merriments Gardens
Hawkhurst Road
Hurst Green
East Sussex TN19 7RA
01580 860666
www.merriments.co.uk

Herbs

Barwinnock Herbs
Barrhill
Ayrshire KA26 0RB
01465 821338
www.barwinnock.com

Hexham Herbs
Chesters Walled Garden
Chollerford
Hexham
Northumberland NE46 4BQ
01434 681483
www.chesterswalledgarden.co.uk

Iden Croft Herbs
Frittenden Road
Staplehurst
Kent TN12 0DH
01580 891432
www.herbs-uk.com

Norfolk Lavender
Caley Mill
Heacham
King's Lynn
Norfolk PE31 7JE
01485 570384
www.norfolk-lavender.co.uk

Rock garden plants and alpines

Birch Farm Nursery
Gravetye
East Grinstead
West Sussex RH19 4LE
01342 810236
www.ingwersen.co.uk

Holden Clough Nursery
Holden
Bolton-by-Bowland
Clitheroe
Lancashire BB7 4PF
01200 447615
www.holdencloughnursery.com

Inshriach Alpine Nursery
Aviemore
Inverness-shire PH22 1QS
01540 651287
www.kincraig.com

Roses

David Austin Roses
Bowling Green Lane
Albrighton
Wolverhampton
West Midlands WV7 3HB
01902 376376
www.davidaustinroses.com

Peter Beales Roses
London Road
Attleborough
Norfolk NR17 1AY
01953 454707
www.classicroses.co.uk

Mattock's Roses
A division of the Notcutts Group,
see Garden Centres for details.
www.mattocks.co.uk

Seed suppliers

Chiltern Seeds
Bortree Stile
Ulverston
Cumbria LA12 7PB
01229 581137
www.chilternseeds.co.uk

Samuel Dobie
Long Road
Paignton
Devon TQ4 7SX
0870 1123623
www.dobies.co.uk

Suttons Seeds
Woodview Road
Paignton
Devon TQ4 7NG
0870 2202899
www.suttons-seeds.co.uk

Thompson & Morgan
Poplar Lane
Ipswich
Suffolk IP8 3BU
01473 588821
www.thompson-morgan.com

Trees and shrubs

Architectural Plants
Cooks Farm
Nuthurst
Horsham
West Sussex RH13 6LH
01403 891772
www.architecturalplants.com

Buckingham Nurseries
Tingewick Road
Buckingham MK18 4AE
01280 822133
www.hedging.co.uk

Unusual perennials

Old Court Nurseries
Colwall
Malvern
Worcestershire WR13 6QE
01684 5404416
www.autumnaster.co.uk

Unusual vegetable seed

Chase Organics
Riverdene Business Park
Molesey Road
Hersham
Surrey KT12 4RG
01932 253666
www.chaseorganics.co.uk

Edwin Tucker
Brewery Meadow
Stonepark
Ashburton
Devon TQ13 7DG
01364 652233
www.edwintucker.com

Seeds-by-Size
45 Crouchfield
Boxmoor
Hemel Hempstead
Hertfordshire HP1 1PA
01442 251458
www.seeds-by-size.co.uk

MATERIALS & TOOLS
General supplies

B & Q
Telephone 0845 3093099 for
your nearest branch.
www.diy.com

Focus
www.focusdiy.co.uk

English Hurdle
Curload
Stoke St. Gregory
Taunton
Somerset TA3 6JD
01823 698418
www.englishhurdle.co.uk

Homebase
0845 0778888
www.homebase.co.uk

Paint and stains

Cuprinol
Wexham Road
Slough
Berkshire SL2 5DS
01753 550555
www.cuprinol.co.uk

Farrow and Ball
Uddens Estate
Wimborne
Dorset BH21 7NL
01202 876141
www.farrow-ball.co.uk

John Oliver
33 Pembridge Road
London W11 3HG
020 7221 6466
www.johnoliver.co.uk

Valtti Specialist Coatings
Unit B3
South Gyle Crescent Lane
Edinburgh EH12 9EG
0131 3344999
www.valtti.co.uk

Planters and garden structures

Anthony de Grey Gardens and Trellises
Broadhinton Yard
77a North Street
London SW4 0HQ
020 7738 8866
www.anthonydegrey.com

Avant Garden
77 Ledbury Road
London W11 2AG
020 7229 4408

Baileys Home and Garden
The Engine Shed
Station Approach
Ross-on-Wye
Herefordshire HR9 7BW
01989 561931
www.baileyshomeandgarden.co.uk

Bulbeck Foundry
Unit 9 Reach Road
Burwell
Cambridgeshire CB5 0AH
01638 743153
www.bulbeckfoundry.co.uk

George Carter
Silverstone Farm
North Elmham
Norfolk NR20 5EX
01362 668130

The Repro Shop
Walcot Reclamation
108 Walcot Street
Bath BA1 5BG
01225 444404
www.walcot.com

Stuart Garden Architecture
Burrow Hill Farm
Wiveliscombe
Somerset TA4 2RN
01984 667458
www.stuartgarden.com

Terracotta and stoneware

Barbary Pots
45 Fernshaw Road
London SW10 0TN
020 7352 1053
www.barbarypots.co.uk

The Chelsea Gardener
125 Sydney Street
London SW3 6NR
020 7352 5656
www.chelseagardener.com

The Conran Shop
Michelin House
81 Fulham Road
London SW3 6RD
020 7589 7401
www.conran.com

Crafts Council Register of Makers
44a Pentonville Road
London N1 9BY
020 7278 7700
www.craftscouncil.org.uk

Crowther at Anthemion
P.O. Box 6
Teddington
Middlesex TW11 0AS
020 8943 4000
www.ornamentalantiques.com

Dorset Reclamation
Cow Drove
Bere Regis
Wareham
Dorset BH20 7JZ
01929 472200
www.dorsetreclamation.co.uk

Wells Reclamation
Coxley
Wells
Somerset BA5 1RQ
01749 677087
www.wellsreclamation.com

Whichford Pottery
Whichford
Nr. Shipston-on-Stour
Warwickshire CV36 5PG
01608 684416
www.whichfordpottery.com

The Willow Pottery
Crossleaze Farm
Bath
Avon BA1 8AU
01225 891919

credits

The authors and publishers would like to thank the people and organizations named below for their contributions to this book.

The garden owners and designers who allowed their gardens to be photographed: Belinda Barnes and Ronald Stuart-Moonlight (Rommany Road, London); Jonathan and Sam Buckley (Barry Road, London); Mr and Mrs David Cargill; Ethne Clarke; Mr and Mrs Robert Clarke; Mike Crosby Jones (Gopsall Pottery, Winchelsea, Sussex); Mr and Mrs Collum (Clinton Lodge, Sussex); Viscount and Viscountess De L'Isle; Mr and Mrs Jeffrey Eker (Old Place Farm, Kent); Gordon Fenn and Raymond Treasure (Stockton Bury, Herts); Major and Mrs Charles Fenwick; Wendy Francis (The Anchorage, West Wickham, Kent); Mrs Clive Hardcastle; Simon and Judith Hopkinson (Hollington Nurseries, Berks); Mr and Mrs Derek Howard; Rosemary Lindsay (Burbage Road, London); Christopher Lloyd (Great Dixter, East Sussex); Janie Lloyd Owen (Eglatine Road, London); Mrs Macleod-Matthews (Chenies Manor, Bucks); Sue Martin (Frittenden, Kent); Dr and Mrs Mitchell (Warren Farm Cottages, Hants); Mr and Mrs Mogford (Rofford Manor, Oxon); David and Mavis Seeney (The Herb Farm, Reading, Berks); The Lady Tollemache; Julian Upston (Cinque Cottage, Ticehurst, East Sussex); Mr and Mrs Williams (Marle Place, Kent); Mr and Mrs Richard Winch; Helen Yemm (Brodrick Road, London).

The owners or managers of: Axletree Garden and Nursery, Peasmarsh, East Sussex; Bates Green, Arlington, East Sussex; Beth Chatto Gardens, Elmstead Market, Essex; Grace Barrand Design Centre, Nutfield, Surrey; The Chelsea Physic Garden, London; Terence Conran's Chef's Garden, RHS Flower Show, Chelsea; Hadspen Garden and Nursery, Castle Cary, Somerset; Hailsham Grange, Hailsham, East Sussex; Hatfield House, Herts; Holkham Hall Garden Centre, Holkham, Norfolk; King John's Lodge, Etchingham, East Sussex; Long Barn, Kent; Marle Place, Brenchley, Kent; Merriments Garden, Hurst Green, East Sussex; Queen Anne's, Goudhurst, Kent; RHS Gardens, Wisley; Royal Botanic Gardens, Kew; Snape Cottage, Chaffeymoor, Dorset; Sticky Wicket Garden, Buckland Newton, Dorset; Upper Mill Cottage, Loose, Kent; West Dean Gardens, Sussex (Edward James Foundation); Whole Earth Foods, Portobello Road, London; Wyland Wood, Robertsbridge, East Sussex.

The photographs on pages 76–77 centre, 94 and 95 were taken by Clive Nichols (Potager-style herb garden with lemon balm in terracotta pot, Chelsea 1993, National Asthma Campaign garden).

Photographs by Jonathan Buckley: pages 5 centre, 7, 8–9 centre, 86, 87, 124, 125, 164 left, 164–165 centre, 166, 167, 174, 175, 178, 179, 182, 183, 194–195 all, 196, 197, 200, 201, 204, 205, 208, 209, 220, 221, 224, 225, 228, 229, 232, 233, 236, 237, 240, 241.

Photographs by Marianne Majerus: pages 2, 5 above and below, 8 left, 9 right, 10, 11, 14, 15, 18, 19, 22, 23, 26, 27, 30, 31, 34, 35, 38, 39, 42, 43, 46–47 all, 48, 49, 52, 53, 56, 57, 60, 61, 64, 65, 68, 69, 72, 73, 77 right, 78, 79, 82, 83, 106 left, 107 right, 116, 117, 120, 121, 128, 129, 144, 145, 148, 149, 152, 153, 156, 157, 190, 191, 212, 213.

Photographs by Stephen Robson: pages 76 left, 90, 91, 98, 99, 102, 103, 106–107 centre, 108, 109, 112, 113, 132, 133, 136, 137, 140, 141, 160, 161, 165 right, 170, 171, 186, 187, 216, 217.

index

acknowledgments

In addition to the owners and establishments mentioned on page 265, the authors would like to thank Jill Duchess of Hamilton for lending urns; Peter Goodwins and Jack Bell for construction and bricklaying; and, for lending plants, Brian and Rosemary Clifton-Sprig, John Powles at the Romantic Garden Nursery, Swannington, Norfolk, and Jane Seabrook and The Chelsea Gardener.

Jane Seabrook also designed two projects: vertical planting on page 120 and the wirework basket on page 156. The brick-edged herb garden (page 78) was designed by Anthony O'Grady, head gardener at Penshurst Place, Kent. The herb-lined pathway (page 94) was designed by Lucy Huntington. All other projects were designed by the authors.

The six titles on which this book is based were edited by Lynn Bryan, Caroline Davison, Toria Leitch, Sarah Polden and Marek Walisiewicz. Graphic design was by Liz Brown, Ingunn Jensen, Mark Latter and Paul Reid. Caroline Davison and Larraine Shamwana helped with photoshoots.